Program Authors

Lindamichelle Baron • Sharon Sicinski-Skeans

Modern Curriculum Press

Parsippany, New Jersey

Special thanks to the following schools for providing student writing samples:

Allendale Elementary School, Oakland, CA

Barbara Bush Elementary School, Houston Independent School District, Houston, TX

Camden Elementary School, Camden, NJ

Center Ridge Elementary School, Centreville, VA

Chattanooga School for Arts and Science, Chattanooga, TN

Clinton Elementary School, Maplewood, NJ

Crown Community Academy, Chicago, IL

Glenwood Elementary School, Short Hills, NJ

Jackson School, Des Moines, IA

Kennedy Elementary School, Santa Ana, CA

Roy Allen Elementary School, Melbourne, FL

Steelton-Highspire Elementary School, Steelton, PA

Wadsworth Elementary School, Chicago, IL

Weslaco ISD, Weslaco, TX

William Halley Elementary School, Fairfax Station, VA

Winston Churchill School, Fairfield, NJ

Project Editors: *Liz Egan-Rivera, Donna Garzinsky* • **Designers:** *Senja Lauderdale, Agatha Jaspon, Dorothea Fox*
Cover Design: *Senja Lauderdale & Chris Otazo* • **Cover Illustration:** *Bernard Adnet*

Acknowledgments

Earth Shine by Anne Morrow Lindbergh. Copyright © 1966, 1969 by Anne Morrow Lindbergh. Reprinted by permission of Anne Morrow Lindbergh.

"Fatherhood" by Thomas Greer. Reprinted by permission of Thomas Greer.

"Harriet Tubman: Antislavery Activist" by M.W. Taylor. Copyright © 1991 by Chelsea House Publishers, a division of Main Line Book Co.

"How To Eat Fried Worms" from *How To Eat Fried Worms and Other Plays* by Thomas Rockwell. Illustrated by Pangid Productions. Text copyright © 1980 by Thomas Rockwell. Illustrations copyright © 1980 by Pangid Productions. Text used by permission of Raines & Raines. Cover used by permission of Dell Books, a division of Bantam Doubleday Dell Publishing Group, Inc.

I Have A Dream by Martin Luther King, Jr. Text copyright © 1963 by Martin Luther King, Jr., copyright renewed 1991 by The Estate of Martin Luther King. Reprinted by arrangement with The Heirs to the Estate of Martin Luther King, Jr., c/o Writers House, Inc. as agent for the proprietor. Cover illustration by Leo and Diane Dillon from *I Have A Dream* by Martin Luther King, Jr. Published by Scholastic Press, a division of Scholastic Inc. Cover illustration © 1997 by Leo and Diane Dillon. Reprinted by permission.

"Layered Liquids" by Julie Agnone from *National Geographic World*, August, 1997. Text and cover reprinted by permission of National Geographic Society.

"Origin of the Ox" from *The Illustrated Book of Myths* by Neil Philip. Illustrated by Nilesh Mistry. Text copyright © 1995 by Neil Philip. Illustrations copyright © 1995 by Nilesh Mistry. Reprinted by permission of Dorling Kindersley Limited.

"Raking It In" by Jennifer Miller from *Girls' Life Magazine* [vol. 4, issue 2]. Text and cover reprinted by permission of *Girls' Life Magazine*.

"The Sidewalk Racer" from *The Random House Book of Poetry for Children* by Jack Prelutsky, illustrated by Arnold Lobel. Copyright © 1983 by Random House, Inc. Text copyright © 1968, 1977 by Lillian Morrison. Text reprinted by permission of Marian Reiner for the author. Cover reprinted by permission of Random House, Inc.

"String and Percussion Instruments" from *The Way Things Work*. Copyright © 1988 by Dorling Kindersley, Ltd. Text copyright © 1988 by David Macaulay and Neil Ardley. Reprinted by permission of Houghton Mifflin Co. and Dorling Kindersley Limited. All rights reserved.

"Dictionary entry" from *Webster's New World Dictionary for Explorers of Language*. Copyright © 1991 by Simon & Schuster. Reprinted with permission of Modern Curriculum Press.

"Who's Following Me?" from *Favorite Scary Stories of American Stories* by Richard and Judy Dockrey Young. Cover design and illustrations by Wendell E. Hall. Text copyright © 1990 by Richard and Judy Dockrey Young. Reprinted by permission of August House Publishers, Inc.

Cursive font used by permission of Zaner-Bloser, Inc.

Art and photo credits appear on page 298.

Modern Curriculum Press

An Imprint of Pearson Learning
299 Jefferson Rd., Parsippany, NJ 07054-0480
www.mcschool.com

ISBN: 0-7652-0752-4

2 3 4 5 6 7 8 9 10   RRD   07 06 05 04 03 02 01 00 99

Contents

Get Ready to Write

The Process of Writing

Are you going in
The Write Direction?

The Forms of Writing

Writer's Handbook

GET READY TO WRITE

Book Tour—A Quick Look

How can this book help you become a better writer?

The Write Direction is full of great ideas about writing. Many of its examples were written by student writers just like you. So if they can improve their writing, you can, too!

This book is divided into four sections.

Get Ready to Write

The five reasons for writing—to learn, to tell a story, to describe, to inform, and to persuade—are introduced in the first unit. You are in this unit now.

The Process of Writing

Here you learn to go through all the stages that successful writers follow when they write. These stages are prewriting, drafting, revising, editing and proofreading, and publishing.

The Forms of Writing

In this unit, you learn about many different forms of writing. You can write your own stories, letters, reports, speeches, and more.

Writer's Handbook

In the first section, Writer's Craft, there are definitions and examples of terms that every writer needs to know. The second section provides practical tips about grammar and usage, mechanics, spelling, and using reference resources.

What are the special features of this book?

Six special features are scattered throughout **The Write Direction**. Page through the book to find examples of each one.

You've got to write to get good at writing. Your Turn gives you a chance to try out what you have just been reading about.

Portfolio

These are reminders to save your writing. They give you opportunities to see how your writing is improving.

Tech Tip

These tips are for when you are writing using a computer. Learn how the computer can help you write.

Think Like a Writer ★ These questions help you connect what you've just learned to your own writing.

Become a Super Writer

These are helpful lessons about an important writing or language skill.

How can you get to know your book?

Look through **The Write Direction**. Read a writing model or a special feature, or check out the *Writer's Handbook* section. Then, use the table of contents and the index to find answers to these questions.

On which pages will you find

- a news story about a natural disaster?
- a concrete poem in the shape of a skateboard?
- a published author's speech?
- writing done by real kids?
- where and when to use *was* and *were*?

Welcome back. You've traveled in **The Write Direction**.

Writer's Tip

These are suggestions from experienced writers. Try each one to see if it works for you.

Writing to Learn

How do you remember what you have learned?

If you take the time to notice, you'll discover that you uncover lots of new information every day.

You learn when you

- read for pleasure.
- watch documentary films on TV.
- work on projects or experiments.
- speak with an expert.

One way to remember the new information you learn is to write it down. You may choose to write a note, to make a list, a chart, or an outline, or to enter something in a log or journal. You are **writing to learn** each time you write to plan, record, remember, organize, list, or ask questions.

> Check your notes just after you write them to be sure they make sense.

Bridges

Suspension Bridges
Old: made of vines and tree trunks
New: made of steel cables suspended between steel or concrete towers

Movable Bridges
Drawbridge: lifts so boats can go underneath

Science

Life Spans

Math

Think Like a Writer

★ What are some ways you can write to learn?

★ When are you writing to learn?

Writing to Tell a Story

What kinds of stories do you like?

Stories involving humor, action-adventure, or mystery are popular favorites. You probably enjoy stories starring kids your own age. These kinds of writing can be entertaining and fun for both the reader and the writer.

How can you write interesting stories for your audience?

If you took a survey, you might find that many kids your age prefer funny stories. Characters who are a lot like the readers themselves are usually high on the list, too. Funny stories with characters your audience can identify with could then be real crowd pleasers.

Think of it. You can draw your audience into a frightening mystery or a science-fiction adventure. These are examples of **writing to tell a story**.

TIM: I heard something!

SAL: *(Sound of a creaking door)* Someone is in the other room.

TIM: Aaaaaagh!

SAL: Run for your life! *(Suddenly the door flings open . . .)*

Play

Traveling forward two thousand years is easy, they were told. As they stepped into the time machine, though, their bodies broke up into tiny particles of light. It had sounded so easy. So why . . .

Science-Fiction Story

Think Like a Writer

★ Do your friends like the same stories that older kids like?

★ How can thinking about your audience help you decide what to write?

Writing to Describe

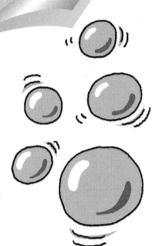

How can you help someone imagine what a person, place, or thing is like?

When you want to tell someone about a person you know, a place you've visited, or something you've received, wouldn't it be wonderful if you had a photograph or brochure? Sometimes you do. Most of the time, though, you use words to **describe in writing** what a person, place, or thing is like.

It is important to paint "word pictures." You want your readers to "see" a person laughing or "hear" the noises of city traffic or "feel" the biting cold water of an ice-covered lake.

How can you create images for your readers?

Vivid words paint vivid images. A puppy that's "soaking wet" is easier to imagine than one that's just "wet." Your audience will get a better mental picture if you also describe how the puppy twisted and rolled in the grass to get dry. Describing how the puppy felt in your hands, the sounds it made, or what it smelled like can paint strong images.

> When I write, I like to tell as much as I can about the way things look, sound, feel, and smell.

> The new girl raced across the schoolyard. She made a full stop just in front of me. Then, as she spun around, she pulled a wandlike object from a tiny jar, and bubbles floated into the air above her. She offered me a turn next.
>
> Description

July 23, 1999

Just my luck! In the morning, the hot sun beat down on me at the beach. Later, I almost drowned in the rain. It rained so hard I could feel the squoosh of water in my shoes as I walked. It sounded funny, too!

Journal

Think Like a Writer

★ What special person or place would you like to describe?

★ What words could you use to describe the way a person laughs?

Writing to Inform

What do you want to know more about?

- The history of your favorite sport
- How kids in other countries live
- The hobbies of American kids, now and long ago

Whenever you find out facts about topics that interest you, you are getting information about them. When you write about those topics, you **write to inform**.

How can you help your audience understand the information you give?

First of all, the facts and ideas must make sense to you or you won't be able to explain them. The facts should be up-to-date and interesting. When you explain how to make or do something, the directions should be clear and in the proper sequence. Here are two examples of writing to inform.

How to Make Fruit Juice

1. Use a big-enough container.
2. Let the frozen juice can thaw until the can gets soft.
3. Open the can and pour the juice into the container.
4. Use the empty juice can to measure and pour in three full cans of water.
5. Put the cover on the container and shake it. If it doesn't have a cover, stir the juice with a large spoon.

Directions

When you think of mummies, you think of Egyptian people who lived thousands of years ago. What you probably don't think of are animal mummies. The ancient Egyptians even mummified cats. The cats weren't pets, though. They were sacred cats. When a sacred cat died, it was mummified ... Research Report

Think Like a Writer
★ What topics are of interest to the kids in your class?
★ How can you share information in an interesting way?

Writing to Persuade

Do you ever want to change the way people think about something?

If you feel strongly about something, you may want to **persuade** others to think as you do. Maybe you want someone to do a favor for you, or perhaps you want to help get a park built in your community. Whatever the topic, you hope the reasons you give will convince your readers.

What will help you to win over your audience to your point of view?

Show respect for your audience. Look at the issue from your audience's point of view. Give reasons that will persuade them. Back up your opinion with facts your readers may not have thought of or known before.

Litter baskets are for litter. Use them and show pride in your school. Don't blame the kids who hang out in the yard after school for the snack wrappers, empty raisin boxes, and juice cans and boxes. Some of us litter at lunch time and before school. Let's all use the new litter baskets and keep the yard clean.

Newspaper Article

39¢   49¢

Have you ever bought something only to find it cheaper somewhere else? That should be your cue to do comparison shopping. How much time could it take you to look for something, such as a video, in more than one store? Just think what you could do with the dollars you save.

Persuasive Paragraph

Think Like a Writer

★ Why should facts relate to your audience's interests?

★ Why would examples based on these facts be convincing?

Writing for Yourself and Others

How are writing for yourself and writing for others different?

Writing for yourself can be like talking to yourself. It's private. It's for you and you alone to read, unless you choose to show it to someone. You can keep a diary and write when you are excited, sad, worried, or even bored. You can make lists in a notebook or draw little cartoons. Writing for yourself can be anything you want it to be.

Sometimes you intend from the start that other people will read what you write. Here are some examples.

- Notes to friends you see every day
- Letters or invitations to friends or family members
- Homework, research reports, stories, book reports
- E-mail messages

Think Like a Writer

★ When might you feel like writing just for yourself?

★ How might writing for yourself improve your writing?

Observing Ants

Monday afternoon

2:00   Placed sugar cube one foot from ant hill.

2:05   Nothing.

2:07   Ant explores sugar cube.

2:20   Ant army pours out of hill.

2:45   Some ants march in straight line back to hill.

Tuesday morning

8:00   Entire cube gone.

Notes

To: kidwizard@moi.com
From: mathwiz@moi.com
Subject: borrowing back my own book
Message:

Dan,

   Please bring my book *Brain Twister Math* to school tomorrow. I really need it.

Angela

E-mail

Planning Your Portfolio

Get organized as a writer.

How can you keep papers from getting lost? One way is to put your writing-in-progress as well as your completed writing in one place. With all of your papers together, you can see how your writing is improving during the school year. A portfolio is a great place to do this.

What's a portfolio?

Portfolio refers to the collection of your writing that can be kept in a binder, a box, a pocket folder, or any other place you choose. A Portfolio logo appears throughout this book to remind you when to save your writing.

Most importantly, your portfolio reminds you and the world that you're a writer. By reviewing your writing over the year, you can better understand the skills you need to work on and see your improvement. You can take pride in what you do well and set goals for what you want to improve.

What can you store in a portfolio?

Since you usually write a piece over many days, it's important to organize your work. When you go through the stages of the writing process, you collect a lot of paper! For longer projects, you may also have notes, index cards, interviews on disk or tape, illustrations and photographs, and charts and diagrams from books, magazines, and the Internet. Keep everything together in your portfolio.

Portfolio

Keep notes, plans, drafts, and final copies of your writing in your portfolio.

The report I wrote this week is so much better than the one I wrote in September!

PORTFOLIO

MY PORTFOLIO

For each writing project, there will be different kinds of papers. Here is a list of the papers you can clip together.

- prewriting and brainstorming notes, such as story maps and outlines
- first draft, with revising and proofreading marks
- photos, drawings, charts, and diagrams
- your final copy

Shown below are the notes, outline, and draft that one writer stores in a section labeled "Work in Progress" in her portfolio. She puts the final copy in a section in the portfolio called "Completed Work."

I. How a roller coaster works
   A. Works without an engine
   B. Cars pulled to top of first hill on chain
   C. Cars unhook from chain and speed faster and faster downhill
II. How a roller coaster uses gravity
   A. Gravity starts the cars moving down the first hill
   B. The height of the first hill and the weight of the cars cause the cars to move faster downhill
   C. Momentum makes the cars go up the next hill. At the same time, gravity is slowing them down

Outline

Trostli, Physics is Fun, Octavo 1995, page 126.
Matter takes up space and has weight.
(matter—roller coaster cars)

Notes

From the way a roller coaster car speeds along the tracks, you might think a roller coaster has an engine. This is not true! A chain in the middle of the track pulls the cars to the top of the first hill.

Draft

Make your own portfolio!

Have you ever set up a portfolio before? If not, your teacher can recommend different ways to set one up. Here are some suggestions to consider.

Get Started

- Use a pocket folder, a large three-ring binder, or a file box in which you can place folders.
- Write your name where it is easy to see.

Consider Organization

Papers stuffed into a portfolio won't be very helpful. The best way to organize a portfolio is to keep it simple.

- A table of contents organized by reasons for writing could be used.
- You might choose to list titles first, and then give the prewriting date and the publishing date.
- Forms of writing is another way to organize your work. Use tabs or labels to separate each form.
- Consider keeping separate sections for works-in-progress and completed works. Other sections can be added at any time.

Think Like a Writer

★ How will keeping a portfolio help you improve your writing?

★ How does keeping a portfolio help you write your final copy?

Portfolio

Make your portfolio large enough to hold all the writing you will do this year.

Choose Your Organization

Organize the contents of your portfolio in a way that makes sense for you. As the year progresses, you will probably have lots of writing in your portfolio, so it's a good idea to use a table of contents. Pick one of the methods suggested on page 12 or use a combination of several of them.

Store your portfolio.

Be sure to store your portfolio in the place in the classroom your teacher has set aside. Check that your name is easily seen.

- Always return your portfolio after each use.
- If you do additional work or research for a project, place the notes, lists, charts, or disks in your portfolio as soon as you can.

Writer's Tip
Write on the Contents page the names of new pieces added to your portfolio. Also, note the publishing date if completed.

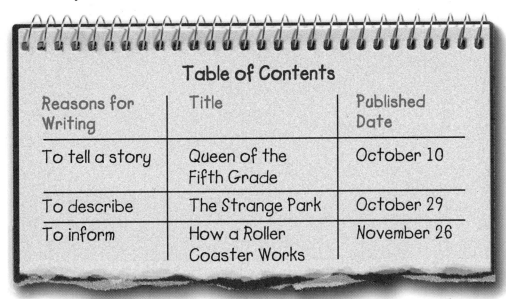

Table of Contents

Reasons for Writing	Title	Published Date
To tell a story	Queen of the Fifth Grade	October 10
To describe	The Strange Park	October 29
To inform	How a Roller Coaster Works	November 26

What can you do with your best writing?

Portfolios can have different purposes. A special showcase portfolio may be used in addition to your regular "working" portfolio. The showcase portfolio is for your best work. At the end of each grading period, your teacher will use this writing to assess your progress as a writer.

Set up your own portfolio. Decide what kind of portfolio you want and how you'll organize it. Choose what works best for you.

Paper, Pen, and Word Processing

How should you prepare first drafts and final copy?

Using a different-colored pencil to make corrections is a big help.

I like to play soccer. I'm on
a ⟨knew⟩ **new** team this year, and
⟨som⟩ **some** of my ⟨freinds⟩ **friends** from
⟨Mountainview⟩ **Mountainview** School are also
on my team.

For Your First Draft

- Write on yellow lined paper for all drafts.
- Write on every other line. This gives you room to add information and make corrections. Use a different-colored pencil to make changes.
- Write on only one side of the paper. That way you can cut, paste, and move paragraphs around if you need to.

For Your Final Copy

- Write your final copy on lined white paper.
- Leave margins of at least one inch at the top, bottom, and both sides of your paper.
- Be sure you have enough time to write your final copy in your best cursive writing.
- Make a new copy if the paper begins to look sloppy.

Think Like a Writer

★ What advantages does a neatly written paper offer to your readers?

Writing my final copy is always fun. Now I get to share what I've written.

Soccer Is Fun
by Jon Niles

I like to play soccer.
I'm on a new team
this year, and some of
my friends from
Mountainview School are
also on my team.

What about writing on a computer?

If you have access to a computer in your classroom, you may be able to do all of your planning and writing by typing on the computer. Here are some word-processing features that you will use regularly.

File   Edit   View   Format   Tools

Name your file
Choose a name that tells what's in the file. For example, FASTRIDE is a better name for a story about roller coasters than RC is.

Save your file
Click on the File menu to learn how your program saves files. Save your writing every five or ten minutes and before you Quit the program.

Type your file
Learn how to use the keyboard with a typing-tutor program. Learn what the special keys, like Backspace, Delete, and Shift, do. Practice using the cursor keys, the F keys, and the mouse or trackball.

Edit your file
Look in the File and Edit menus. Usually you can Copy, Cut and Paste text, Find and Replace text, and Undo what you just did.

Check the spelling
Your word-processing program probably has a spell-checking tool. Read the choices you are given carefully. Pick the word that has the meaning you want.

Print your file
To print, click on an icon or choose Print from the File menu. Always Save and Print a copy of your work before you Close the file or before you Quit, or exit, the program.

Think Like a Writer

★ In what other ways can a computer help you with your writing?

Computer Keyboard

THE PROCESS OF WRITING

The Stages in the Process

Writing is a way to communicate ideas and feelings. You might write entries in a journal or diary, or you might send a letter or an E-mail or prepare a report. These are just some of the things you probably write.

Most writing involves thinking, planning, and putting your ideas on paper. It also involves making changes to improve what you have written. That is why most writers talk about writing as a process.

Here are the stages that many people use when they write.

1. Prewriting

Prewriting is planning and getting ready to write.

- Brainstorm and get ideas.
- Select a topic.
- Gather information and ideas.
- Make a writing plan for what to say and how to say it.

5. Publishing

Publishing is sharing your work with others. You can share your work in many ways. Here are a few ideas.

- Write a paper or a report.
- Send a letter or an E-mail.
- Make a book.
- Tell a story.
- Put on a play.
- Give a speech.
- Make a video recording.

2. Drafting

Drafting is putting your ideas down on paper.

- Use your writing plan as a guide.
- Let your ideas flow.
- Keep writing without stopping to correct grammar or spelling.

3. Revising

Revising is changing and improving your writing.

- Read over your writing with "fresh eyes."
- Make sure you followed your writing plan.
- Talk with other people about your writing.

4. Editing and Proofreading

Editing and proofreading is checking your writing one last time.

- Read your revised work carefully.
- Look for mistakes in grammar and usage, capitalization, abbreviation, punctuation, and spelling.
- Make a clean copy of your work.
- Proofread your writing to correct any mistakes you might have missed.

Think Like a Writer

★ Why would writers want to go back to an earlier stage of writing?

Prewriting

Think It Through

Prewriting is the beginning of the writing process. It is your time for thinking, selecting a writing topic, gathering ideas, and organizing your information. It's also when you start to think about your audience, your purpose for writing, and the form your writing will take. Another thing you do during prewriting is make a plan. That plan will help you stay organized and focused when you begin to write.

Brainstorming

Brainstorming is one way to get ideas for writing. When brainstorming, you just let ideas pop into your mind, one idea after another. Soon, you will have lots of ideas to choose from for your writing. To brainstorm, you

- list things you know or do or have read about lately.
- do a quick write about one topic. Keep writing until you run out of ideas.
- talk with people about what you've done and read.
- check your journal or log for interesting ideas.
- "see" a picture in your mind, quickly draw it on paper, and then describe its details in words.

Here's a list I brainstormed about things I like to do.

What I Like

Exploring new places

Hiking

Watching movies about exciting adventures

White-water rafting

List

1. Exploring new places
2. Hiking
3. Horseback riding
4. Visiting the Grand Canyon
5. Camping

Story Ideas

Think Like a Writer

★ Why do you think writers might work with partners when they brainstorm?

Select a Topic

After you brainstorm, you will have lots of ideas for your writing. Now it is time to select one of them to write about.

Start by looking over your ideas. Then write these sentence beginnings on a sheet of paper and complete them.

- The topic I like the best is _____.

- The topic I know the most about is _____.

- The topic other people will want to read about

  most is _____.

When you have chosen your topic, finish the sentence below. Refer to it from time to time to remind yourself about your subject, audience, purpose, and form of writing.

I am writing this _report_ about _the Grand Canyon_
             form   subject

to _share information about Grand Canyon wildlife_
                       purpose

with my classmates .
        audience

Gather and Organize Information

Once you have selected your topic, you can start to gather ideas and information.

- Write down any questions you have as well as any ideas and facts you already know about the topic.

- Get answers to questions you don't know by reading or observing and taking notes.

- Make a chart to gather and organize your information.

Read the examples below and on the next page.

Clusters

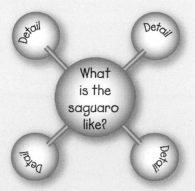

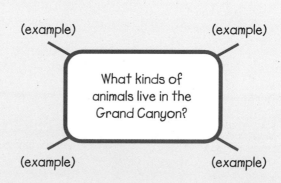

More Ways to Gather and Organize Information

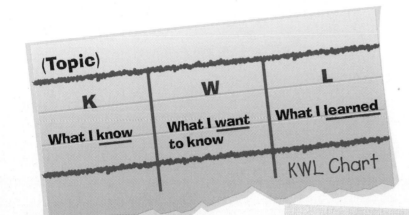

(Topic)		
K	**W**	**L**
What I know	What I want to know	What I learned

KWL Chart

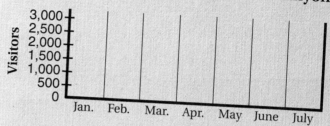

Number of Visitors to the Grand Canyon

Graph

(TOPIC)

Questions	Information From				
	Books	Magazines	Videos	Web Sites	Interviews
1.					
2.					
3.					

Gathering Chart

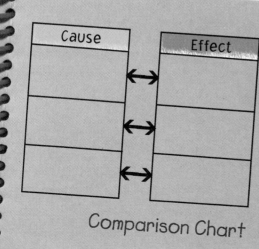

Cause	Effect

Comparison Chart

Think Like a Writer

★ What questions do you think you should ask yourself as you look for information?

Design a Plan

Now it is time to create a plan for your writing. There are several kinds of plans you can use. The one you use will depend on the form of writing that you are doing. Your plan will help keep you focused on these questions.

Subject: What am I writing about?

Purpose: Why am I writing?

Audience: Who will read my writing?

Form: What kind of writing is it?

Writer's Tip
Speak with a partner about your plan. Consider your partner's suggestions about ideas that could be added or taken out.

Beginning
(Introduce main characters, setting, and theme.)

Middle
(Tell events in a logical order.)

End
(Tell how everything works out.)

Story Map

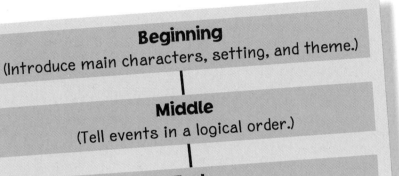

DIFFERENT

(Topic) **ALIKE** (Topic)

Venn Diagram

① → ② → ③ → ④ → ⑤ → ⑥ → ⑦

Beginning   Middle   End

Time Line

(Topic)
　I. (Main Idea)
　　A. (Example)
　　B. (Example)
　　　1. (Detail)
　　　2. (Detail)
　II. (Main Idea)
　　A. (Example)
　　　1. (Detail)
　　　2. (Detail)

Outline

Think Like a Writer

★ How can a time line help you plan for writing about an event or something that happened in history?

Put It Into Words

Once you have finished your writing plan, you can begin writing, or drafting, as it is called. Sometimes you will want to get more facts or add a new item to your plan. Remember, you can always return to prewriting while you are drafting.

Write a First Draft

Drafting is getting your ideas down on paper—any way you can. When you write a first draft, you simply look over your writing plan, gather your thoughts together, and then start writing.

- Let your ideas flow onto the page.
- Try out different ideas and words. Later, if you don't like them, you can change them.
- Don't worry about grammar or spelling. You can fix mistakes later.
- Just write . . . write . . . write.

See the outline that's the writing plan for the draft below.

Writer's Tip
Most writers review their information, and then concentrate on just getting their ideas on paper when they draft.

I. Grand Canyon Wildlife
   A. Over 250 kinds of birds
   B. Many other creatures
      1. Deer, antelopes, bears, bighorn sheep, prairie dogs
      2. Snakes, lizards, scorpions
II. Grand Canyon Plants
   A. Bottom of the canyon
      1. Cactuses
      2. Yuccas, mesquite, agaves

Outline

Many kinds of wildlife live in the Grand Canyon. To begin with, there are over 250 kinds of birds that live there. There also are other creatures. Some are common, such as deer, antelopes, bears, bighorn sheep, and prairie dogs. Animals like snakes, lizards, and scorpions live at the bottom of the canyon.

Draft

Think Like a Writer
★ Why do you think many writers skip lines when they write their first drafts?

Subject, Audience, and Purpose

Keep your subject in mind as you write your first draft. Ask yourself: Do these facts or details relate to my topic? For example, you wouldn't write about wildlife in Yellowstone in a research report on wildlife in the Grand Canyon.

Also think about your audience. Your goal is to write what your audience needs to know or will be interested in reading.

Your purpose is your reason for writing. You could be writing to tell a story, to describe something, to inform someone about something, or to persuade someone to your point of view.

Think Like a Writer
* ★ How is writing that tells a story different from writing that informs?
* ★ How is writing that describes something different from writing that persuades?

Forms of Writing

There is a form of writing to match every purpose for writing. As you write, remind yourself of the form of writing you are using: Is it a play, a story, or a poem? Think about what that form is like and how it looks on the page. Ask yourself:

* Am I sticking to my form of writing?
* Is this the best form of writing to use for what I want to write?

Remember, you are only writing a draft. You can change anything—even your form of writing—if you need to.

Conferencing

Have you ever gotten "stuck" not knowing what to write next? One way to get "unstuck" is to have a conference with your partner or partners. Focus on your topic and then try talking through what you want to say. Ask for suggestions. Listen to your partners' ideas, take notes, and decide which ideas to include.

Revising is the third stage in the writing process. In some ways, it is like a store's returns department because you can exchange what you have for something else. In writing, you can "return" your work and redo parts or all of it.

Revising gives you, the writer, the opportunity to change your mind. You can change the order of your ideas, exchange or replace a word with a better one, and correct facts and details, all to make your writing better. That is why revising is so important to writers.

Check Information

When you revise, you check the information in your writing. Look back over your notes and your writing plan. Check that

- everything important is included.
- all information supports the main idea.
- the information is correct.
- the ideas are stated clearly.

Check Organization

Revising is also the time when you check that your writing is well organized. Your writing should have a clear beginning, middle, and end. Think about the following questions.

- Does the beginning tell about my topic and get the reader interested?
- Do the ideas presented in the middle explain the topic?
- Does the end include a closing idea about the topic?

Stay Focused

Make sure your writing is still focused on your topic. Revising gives you a chance to change anything that does not suit your audience or your reason for writing. Be sure to

- look for missing details or ideas that do not relate.
- speak to the same audience in every part of your work.
- use the same point of view or voice in your writing.

Revising Marks

≡	capitalize
⋀	add
✄	remove
⊙	add a period
/	make lowercase
⌒	move
∿	transpose

Many kinds of wildlife live in the Grand Canyon. To begin with, there are over 250 kinds of birds thrive within the canyon's walls. that live there. There also are other creatures. Some are common, such as deer, antelopes, bears, bighorn sheep, and prairie dogs. Animals like snakes, lizards, and scorpions live at the bottom of the canyon.

Add a descriptive detail to expand sentence.

Replace a word with a better one.

Check Language

Revising also gives you the chance to improve your use of language. Your choice of words can help your audience understand what you are trying to communicate. Ask yourself the following questions.

- Should I be using formal or informal language?
- Are there other words that would make my ideas easier to understand?
- Is there a synonym that would catch the reader's attention?
- Are there sensory words that would help the reader see, hear, smell, or taste what I am writing about?

Conferencing

After you finish revising your work, read it aloud to a partner or small group of classmates. Ask for comments as well as suggestions about how to improve what you have written. A partner often notices things in your writing that you may have missed. Listen to your partner's ideas, take notes about them, and then respond to the ideas.

Conferencing Checklist

- Do I keep to my topic?
- Do my ideas make sense?
- Do I tell things in the right order?
- Is my writing smooth and pleasant to read?
- What can I do to make my writing better?

Think Like a Writer

★ Why might you revise your work more than once?

Polish Your Writing

This is the stage for fixing mistakes in grammar, usage, capitalization, punctuation, and spelling. Read your writing several times. Look for a different kind of mistake each time. Mark your corrections with Proofreading Marks.

Grammar and Usage

To check your grammar and usage, proofread your writing for incorrectly formed sentences and paragraphs. Also check the eight parts of speech. Here are several examples.

Writer's Tip
As you edit, use the Grammar and Usage section in the *Writer's Handbook*, on pages 241–264.

- Every sentence has a subject and a predicate.
  The canyon is a popular tourist destination.

- Irregular nouns do not form the plural with *s* or *es*.
  Two men are hiking the Kaibab Trail.

- Verbs agree with their subjects.
  Many visitors come to the canyon in the spring.

- Pronouns agree with their antecedents.
  The prairie dog scurried into its burrow.

- Adjectives are used properly to describe nouns.
  The air in the canyon is hot.

- Adverbs are used properly to describe adjectives.
  The air in the canyon is very hot in the summer.

- Prepositions relate nouns to other words.
  Sometimes, there is snow on the North Rim in the winter.

- Conjunctions join two or more words, phrases, or simple sentences.
  Scorpions and snakes live in the lower canyon.

- Interjections are followed by exclamation points or commas.
  Wow! Did you see that? Hey, it's a real mountain lion.

Mechanics

After you have read and corrected any grammar and usage errors, read your work again. This time, correct errors in capitalization and punctuation—the mechanics of writing.

Capitalization

First, check your writing for words that should be capitalized—proper nouns, proper adjectives, titles, abbreviations, and the first word of a sentence. At the same time, check for words that do not need capital letters.

The first europeans to see the Grand Canyon arrived in 1540. They were part of francisco Coronado's Expedition that explored much of southwestern North America.

CORONADO

Punctuation

Next, check your work for punctuation errors. Here are just a few things to look for.

- Periods or question marks at the ends of sentences and periods in abbreviations
  Grand Canyon National Park was set up by the U.S. Congress in 1919. Do you know which national parks are older?

- Commas between items in a list
  Horses, donkeys, and mules travel through the canyon.

- Apostrophes in contractions and words that show possession
  Isn't Mike's cap green?

- Quotation marks around a speaker's exact words
  "Wait," she said. "We'll leave in a moment."

Spelling

Always proofread your writing for spelling errors.

mountain lions   bear
In one part of the canyon, you can see mountan liyuns and bare.

See page 31 for some tips to help you check words you are not sure how to spell.

- Check to see if the word was used in your information sources.

- Look up the word in a dictionary. For most words, you may need to try many different spellings until you find the word.

- Keep a personal spelling dictionary and refer to it when you write. A personal spelling dictionary contains new words that you encounter and words that usually give you trouble. Look the words over every once in a while.

- If you did your work on a computer, you can use the spell-checking tool in your word-processing program.

For more help with spelling, see the *Writer's Handbook* section, on pages 275–284.

Appearance

Once you have finished editing and proofreading your work, make a neat final copy of it. Work slowly. Make sure that you don't leave out any information. Be sure to give your writing a title that works for your topic and that will grab your audience.

Use your best penmanship. Make sure everything looks right on the page and that you have followed instructions about margins. They are the spaces at the top, bottom, and sides of your page. If you are using a computer, use a font—a style of type—that will be easy to read.

Proofreading Marks

Mark	Meaning
⌐	indent first line of paragraph
≡	capitalize
∧ or ∨	add
ℐ	remove
⊙	add a period
/	make lowercase
◯	spelling mistake
⌒	move
∾	transpose

Think Like a Writer

★ Why do you think writers wait until the editing and proofreading stage to fix errors in grammar, usage, mechanics, and spelling?

Share Your Work

Most writers plan from the start to share their writing with others. They plan, revise, and proofread their writing so they can publish it. Publishing is the last stage in the writing process.

Publishing can take various forms. Which ones have you used to share your writing with a friend, a classmate, or a family member?

On Tuesday morning, we rode out to one of the ridges. It was awesome!

See It in Print

Books

You can easily put your writing into a book, because books come in all shapes and sizes. Draw pictures or use photos to illustrate what you have written. Then, fasten the pages and attach a cover.

Magazines and Newspapers

Magazines and newspapers are popular ways to publish. Maybe you and your classmates can publish a class magazine to share your writing. Be creative.

Visuals almost always help your audience get a better picture of what you are saying. Here are some reasons for adding visuals.

- **Illustrations:** Photos and drawings let readers see what you are writing about. They make your writing come alive.

- **Graphs:** Changes or differences often make more sense when they're plotted on a graph. Graphs help your readers see how things change or differ over time.

- **Charts:** Tables and lists let your readers compare facts and figures.

> ### A Different Approach
> Try other ways to publish your writing.
> - Bulletin boards
> - E-mail
> - Posters
> - Letters

Hear It Live or on Tape

You can also share your ideas or information in person or on tape. You still follow all the stages of the writing process when you do this, but you share your work with spoken words instead of printed ones.

Presentations

- In an oral report, you share information with your audience about a topic you've studied.
- A speech is a good way to share your ideas and opinions if you want to persuade your audience to think or act in a certain way.

Performances

- When you tell a story, you present it with as much drama and expression as possible. Props and music can be added to dress up your performance.
- Recording your writing on videotapes or audiotapes allows you to do long-distance publishing or to give repeat performances.

Use Technology

Whether you publish your writing in print or before a live audience, using a computer can help you. Here are some of the things you can do with a computer.

- Make drawings to illustrate your work.
- Include pictures and illustrations that you get from computer programs and the Internet.
- Dress up your cover with fonts in different sizes, shapes, and colors.
- Print several copies with a click of the mouse.
- Store your work for safekeeping.

Reporting live from the Grand Canyon . . .

Tech Tip
Use different type styles and background patterns to vary the look of your pages.

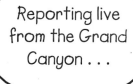

Think Like a Writer
- ★ How do you decide which is the best way to publish?
- ★ How have you published your writing? Which way do you like the most?

THE FORMS OF WRITING

TAKE NOTE

Writing to Learn

Writing Notes and Lists

Perhaps you've seen reporters, pilots, or scientists in movies, or maybe you've observed store owners and police officers as they work. They take **notes** and make **lists** so that they can remember information and use it later.

Recording information is one way to learn new ideas and remember details. As you read for reports and other assignments, take notes on index cards or type them on the computer. At the top of each note, add the name of the book and the page number.

From <u>Thomas Jefferson and His World</u>, p. 73

Inventor
- writing machine that copied letters
- folding ladder
- chair that turned around
  on its base

Notes

Lists are another helpful writing tool. They are especially useful for brainstorming, expanding, and organizing ideas and details.

Kinds of Chairs
swivel chairs
wooden chairs
metal chairs
upholstered chairs
wheelchairs
reclining chairs
folding chairs

List

Talk About the Models

★ Why did the writer put only one idea on the card?

★ Why does the writer write his source on the card?

★ How can the writer use the list to get ideas for his report?

Meet the Writer

When I read and take notes, I paraphrase the important ideas. That means I write them down in my own words. Then, I put my note cards in an order that makes sense.

Chris Wen
New Mexico

Your Turn

Write notes for a social studies project or another project you are working on.

● Record each important idea on a card.

● Write the source of your information.

● Include a page number for the source.

Writing Log Entries

Keeping a **log** is a great way to sort out your thoughts and feelings about a book you've read. It can also help you remember what you are learning and can be used to record observations.

A log can be made from a tabbed notebook or binder. It is divided into three sections: Literature Log, Learning Log, and Observation Log.

Literature Log

In your **Literature Log**, you can write about a story, its characters, and what's interesting about the story's beginning, middle, and end. Include several entries for each story. As you read, you may be reminded of things in your own life or in other books. The entries in your Literature Log can give you ideas for your writing.

> The Adventures of Tom Sawyer,   Nov. 12
> Chapter 1, by Mark Twain
>
> Main Character: Tom Sawyer
> What he is like:
> - adventurous, likes to break rules, seems like a daredevil
> - enjoys the outdoors
> - teases other boys
> - likes pretty girls   Literature Log

Talk About the Model

★ How does this writer respond to the story she read?

★ How can this entry help her come up with ideas for her own writing?

Learning Log

Use the **Learning Log** section of your notebook for school subjects. Label tabs *Math*, *Social Studies*, *Science*, and *Language Arts*. Add other tabs if you need them.

Write down everything you want to remember about each school subject. What you write about one subject can sometimes help you with another subject. Also, write any questions you have. Your questions can help you focus on what you need to learn.

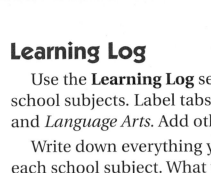

Sept. 12

Today, I have these questions about rivers in my state:
- Where are they located?
- Where do they begin and end?
- How do people use them?

My ideas:
- logging, fishing, kayaking, boating, skiing, rafting, ice skating, swimming

River	Location	Activity

Oct. 23

Today, I learned about measurements.

12 inches = 1 foot

3 feet = 1 yard

5,280 feet = 1 mile

1,760 yards = 1 mile

144 square inches = 1 square foot

9 square feet = 1 square yard

I still have these questions:

Learning Log

Writer's Tip
Your Learning Log can be a great place to record facts and to find ideas for writing.

Talk About the Models

★ Why did the writer use a chart as part of her log entry on rivers?

★ How might the writer use her facts, ideas, and questions?

Observation Log

Writer's Tip
Write in your Observation Log every day. Being aware of the world around you can help you become a better writer.

Use the last section of your notebook as an **Observation Log**. Record vivid details about things that you can see, hear, smell, taste, and feel. You may want to write down what you are doing in math class, your step-by-step observations from a science experiment, or notes about something you observed in person, such as a baseball game. Later on, your observations can give you ideas to write about or details to add to your writing.

Date and Time: May 3, 1:00 p.m.
Place: Baseball field at school
What happened:
- Crowd was quiet
- Dawn came up to bat.
- 1st swing—strike
- 2nd swing-center field fly ball
- Crowd cheered and roared
- Dawn rounded the bases, made team's first home run

Observation Log

Talk About the Model

★ When might this observation be useful to the writer?

★ What details does the writer include that can be checked for accuracy?

★ What details could be used later as ideas for writing?

Make your own log.
- Divide a notebook into three sections, using paper or plastic tabs.
- Label the sections *Literature Log*, *Learning Log*, and *Observation Log*. In your Learning Log, make separate sections for each school subject.
- Date each entry that you make.

Writing Journal Entries

Do you know anyone who keeps a journal? A **journal** is a place to write down anything from the day's events to special experiences or future plans. Your journal is just for you, so write about whatever is important to you. Try to write in it every day, and always date your entry so that you can remember when the event happened.

Meet the Writer

I divide my journal into different sections. One section is for quick writing. That's where I write anything about a topic that pops into my mind.

Alberto Nunez
Colorado

April 10

> I was digging in my backyard to plant some flower seeds. My shovel hit something that sounded like metal. I dug around carefully with my hands, and there was a coin. It was covered with dirt and hard to read. Dad and I cleaned it off. It was a very old nickel with a buffalo on one side. I will add it to my coin collection.

Journal Entry

Talk About the Model

★ What event did the writer record in this entry?

★ Why did the writer record this event in his journal instead of his log?

Your Turn

Create your own journal.

- Buy a diary or notebook to use as a journal.
- Think about what you want to note in your journal. Use quick writing to help you.
- Write about the experiences, memories, ideas, plans, and feelings that are important to you.
- Include dates, descriptions, and sketches for each entry.

Writing Paragraphs

Imagine how hard it would be to read two, three, four—or forty—pages of writing with no break. You'd have a hard time figuring out the writer's meaning. That's why writers use paragraphs. A **paragraph** is a group of sentences that tell about a single idea.

- A **narrative paragraph** tells a story, presenting events in the order that they happened.

- A **descriptive paragraph** tells what a person, a place, a thing, or an idea is like.

- An **expository paragraph** gives directions or explains information.

- A **persuasive paragraph** presents reasons, arguments, and opinions to win over the reader to a certain point of view.

The topic sentence tells readers the main idea of a paragraph. It is usually the first sentence, but sometimes it's found in the middle or at the end of a paragraph. Sometimes, the topic sentence can be more than one sentence. The rest of the sentences in a paragraph are detail, or supporting, sentences.

Topic sentence

I had a wonderful time when I visited my grandparents' farm last weekend. First, Grandma let me milk one of the cows. After that, Grandpa took me out to plow a field on his tractor. He even let me sit in the driver's seat when the engine was off. On Sunday, we went fishing after doing our chores. I hated to leave when the weekend was over.

Paragraph

Detail, or supporting, sentences

The information you give about your main idea should be written in an **order** that makes sense. You can write information in the order in which things happen, using words such as *first*, *next*, *then*, and *last*. This is called **time order**. Tommy wrote his paragraph on page 42, using time order.

Another way to write about something is to use **spatial order**. With spatial order, you describe something from front to back, top to bottom, left to right, and so on.

My grandparents' farm is not very big. Their house is next to the front gate. Behind the house is a barn for the cows and a shed for the tractors. Right behind the barn are two tall blue silos, where food for the cows is kept.

Spatial Order

You can also put information in **order of importance.** To do this, start with the most important event or thing and end with the least important.

I had a wonderful time at the farm last weekend. The most fun I had was going fishing. I caught the only fish. I also enjoyed milking one of the cows by hand. Grandma told me I did a good job. Another thing I did was ride on the tractor with Grandpa.

Order of Importance

Talk About the Models

★ What kind of paragraph did Tommy write on page 42—narrative, descriptive, expository, or persuasive?

★ What words show time order in that paragraph?

★ What words show spatial order in the first model above?

★ What words show order of importance in the second model?

Your Turn

Choose one type of paragraph to write. Find a topic to write about in your journal or log.

- Decide which order you want to use.
- Write a topic sentence that tells what the paragraph is about.
- Add sentences with supporting details.

Writing Summaries and Paraphrases

Meet the Writer

I write a summary when I look up information on the Internet or when I use a book in the library. That way, I'll always have the important information I found.

Darlene Lee
Florida

For some writing projects, you'll need to collect lots of information. To help you understand and remember that information, summarize it. A **summary** combines the important ideas of a chapter or an article into one clear paragraph. To summarize, write the main idea in your own words in the first sentence. Add important facts or details.

from *The Way Things Work* by David Macaulay

Percussion instruments are struck, usually with sticks or mallets, to make a sound. Often the whole instrument vibrates and makes a crack or crash, as in castanets and cymbals. Their sound does not vary in pitch and can only be made louder or softer. Drums contain stretched skins, which may vibrate to give a pitched note. As with strings, tightening the skin makes the note higher in pitch and smaller drums give higher notes.

Tuned percussion instruments, such as the xylophone, have sets of bars that each give a definite note. The pitch of the note depends on the size of the bar, a smaller bar giving a higher pitch.

Original Text

The Way Things Work
by David Macaulay
You hit a percussion instrument to make a sound. Castanets and cymbals make only one sound. Drums can make different sounds. It depends on the size of the drum. A xylophone makes real notes, depending on the size of the bar.

Summary

Talk About the Model

★ What was the main idea of the original text?

★ Does the writer's summary give a clear picture of the important ideas in the article from *The Way Things Work*?

When you do research, you sometimes want to copy down a writer's exact words so that you can quote what the writer said. Most of the time, though, you read mainly to get information. In this case, it helps to **paraphrase** the information. To paraphrase, use your own words, not the writer's, to write down information.

Jogging is one of today's most popular forms of exercise. One reason why people jog is that jogging does not require expensive equipment. Joggers need only shorts, T-shirts, sweat suits, or just about any other clothes that fit loosely. The only item that any jogger needs to buy is a good pair of running shoes.

Magazine Article

Writer's Tip
In a chapter or article, the first few sentences in each paragraph often give the most important ideas.

People like to jog because they don't need a lot of expensive equipment, just running shoes and loose-fitting, comfortable clothes.

Paraphrase

Talk About the Model

★ Does this paraphrase give the most important ideas of the paragraph? Why or why not?

Your Turn

Find a magazine or encyclopedia article about a topic that interests you.

- Write a paraphrase of the opening paragraph. Use your own words to write the important ideas.
- Write a summary of the rest of the article. Note the main idea, add important details, and arrange the facts in an order that makes sense.

Using Organizers, Diagrams, Outlines, Graphs, and Charts

Meet the Writer

I use cluster diagrams a lot when I prewrite. I can see at a glance how ideas are connected. I can also see if I've left out anything important.

Alan Tramm
Mississippi

As you gather information for your writing, you will need to organize it. When you share your work, you may want to present some information in a visual way. This can help your readers understand your facts more easily.

Organizers, Diagrams, and Outlines

Organizers, diagrams, and outlines can help you get ready to write by grouping your information in a way that makes sense for the form of writing you are doing. Some can also help you share your work because they can explain or present your facts better than just words can.

- A **cluster** shows the connection between a main idea and its supporting details.

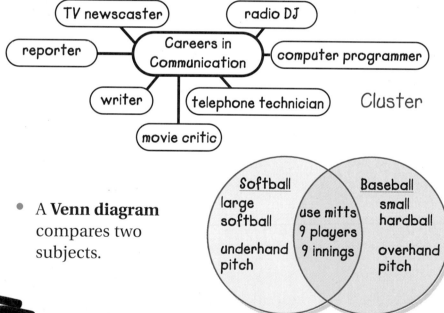

Cluster

- A **Venn diagram** compares two subjects.

Venn Diagram

- A **time line** shows the order in which events take place.

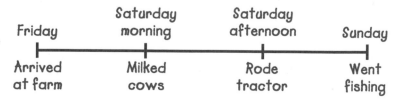

Time Line

- An **inverted triangle** shows information from most important to least important or from most general to most specific.

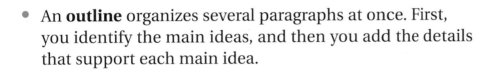

Lunar Prospector
reaches moon.

North and south poles
are mapped.

Surface is tested
with spectrometer.

Ice is found
in polar
craters.

Inverted Triangle

- An **outline** organizes several paragraphs at once. First, you identify the main ideas, and then you add the details that support each main idea.

Immigrants to the United States

I. In the past

   A. From Western Europe

   B. From Eastern Europe

II. In the present

   A. From Central and South America

   B. From Asia

Outline

Writer's Tip

Diagrams can show how something works or is made. Use the diagram that works best for the writing you're doing.

Talk About the Models

★ How does a cluster help the writer organize ideas?

★ When might the writer use a Venn diagram?

Use an organizer to gather and present ideas and information.

- Select a fun topic to write about.
- Think about the kinds of information you can gather for this topic.
- Choose the organizer that will work best.

Graphs and Charts

Graphs and charts can help you make sense of the information you collect. They are also a good way to share facts and information with your readers. Information often is clearer when it is presented visually.

A pie chart can show how parts relate to a whole.

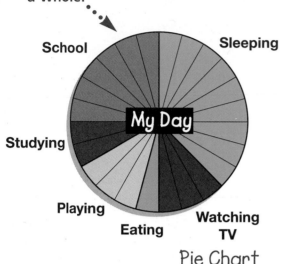

Pie Chart

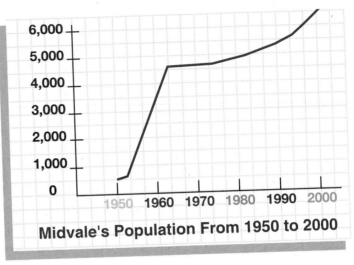

Midvale's Population From 1950 to 2000

Line Graph

A line graph can show how something changes over a period of time.

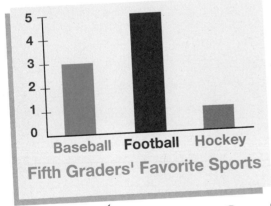

Fifth Graders' Favorite Sports

Bar Graph

A bar graph can compare several things at a particular point in time.

Talk About the Models

★ How does the line graph show changes in the population from 1950 to 2000?

★ Why did the writer use a pie chart instead of a bar graph to show his different activities during one day?

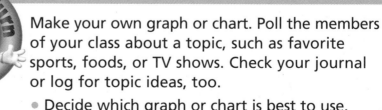

Your Turn

Make your own graph or chart. Poll the members of your class about a topic, such as favorite sports, foods, or TV shows. Check your journal or log for topic ideas, too.

● Decide which graph or chart is best to use.

● Create it as accurately as you can.

● Plot the results of your poll.

ONCE UPON A TIME

Writing to Tell a Story

Writing a Narrative Paragraph

Meet the Writer

I wrote this paragraph because I know a lot of families move, and kids feel sad about it.

Linda Ocasio
Texas

Have you ever wanted to share some news with a friend, a relative, or a classmate? A **narrative paragraph** tells about an event in the writer's life. "Moving On" is about the day Linda's family packed up to move to Texas. Linda's details about packing the breakfast dishes and watching her father and brothers pack the truck make her experience come alive for the reader.

Moving On
by Linda Ocasio

I live in Texas now. I'm surrounded by wide-open spaces and a sky that goes on forever. From the time I was a baby, though, my family and I lived in a small apartment in Philadelphia. I knew we were finally going to move when we washed our breakfast dishes and packed them in a box. When my father pulled the van up in front of our building, that was the first box he and my brothers took. The three of them soon were hauling beds and chairs and tables out the door. Piece by piece our furniture disappeared inside the truck. I felt sad and lost when the last of our belongings was loaded into the truck. Then it hit me. A new part of my life was beginning. It was time to be moving on.

124

Talk About the Model

★ How does the writer get you involved in her story?

★ The last sentence is the topic sentence. Why might the writer have chosen to end with the topic sentence?

★ Which details make the characters and setting come alive?

Make a Plan

Now it's your turn. Start by planning what you will write.

• Make a list of events in your life that you might like to share with others.

• Choose an event that you can tell about in one paragraph.

• Jot down details that will help bring the event to life.

Write It Down

• Write an opening sentence that will catch your reader's attention. Be sure to indent.

• Write in the first person, using *I* and *me*.

• Use strong action verbs and describing words to help readers see and feel what is happening.

• Tell the events in the order they happened.

Conferencing

Read your narrative paragraph to a partner. Is he or she able to explain the main idea? Does he or she get a clear picture of the characters and setting?

Look It Over

Read your paragraph aloud. Did you tell the story clearly and accurately? Are the details in order? Are any details missing? Did you use *I* and *me* correctly? Is your spelling correct?

Tech Tip

If your word processor has a Thesaurus tool, use it to find strong action verbs and vivid describing words.

Portfolio

Store your narrative paragraph. Later, you may want to compare it with other narrative writings you do.

Writing Jokes, Puns, and Terse Verse

Meet the Writer

I love making people laugh. My friends say that someday I'll have my own comedy show on TV. I hope they're right.

Kenneth Johnson
Maryland

Humorous writing is a popular kind of writing. Jokes are a good example. **Jokes** arc things that people say, do, or write to amuse people or make them laugh. **Puns,** plays on words, and **terse verse,** two rhyming words that describe a subject, are other examples.

To write humor, writers pick subjects and situations that they think will be funny. Kenneth likes to write jokes, puns, and terse verse. Here are some of his favorites.

A penguin walks into a drugstore and asks for some lip balm. The sales clerk hands it over, and the penguin replies, "Please put it on my bill."

Joke

This is a humorous story. The joke ends with a punch line.

"Are 12-legged, orange caterpillars with short, black hair good to eat?" asked Ben at breakfast.

"No," said his dad. "Why do you ask?"

"Well," replied Ben, "there was one in your cereal, but now its gone."

Joke

There is a humorous answer to the question.

Talk About the Jokes

As a Reader

★ Are Kenneth's jokes funny? Why or why not?

★ How are these jokes like stories?

As a Writer

★ Where do you think Kenneth got ideas for his jokes?

★ How can the punch line help you to write a joke?

Knock, knock.
Who's there?
Lettuce.
Lettuce who?
Lettuce in.
It's cold outside.

Pun

The words *lettuce* and *let us* sound almost the same.

Two-knee fish and *tuna fish* sound almost the same.

Most fish have two eyes and two fins. But what would you call a fish that has two knees?

A two-knee fish

Pun

Talk About the Puns

As a Reader

★ What makes the puns funny?

★ What words are the puns based on?

As a Writer

★ How is a pun like a joke?

★ Do you think the writer started with a funny idea or with two words that sound almost the same?

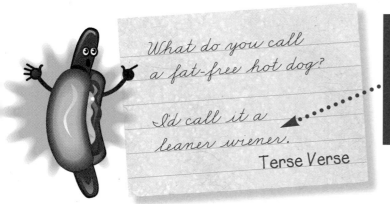

What do you call a fat-free hot dog?

I'd call it a leaner wiener.

Terse Verse

Two rhyming words sum up the subject.

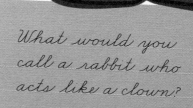

Talk About the Terse Verse

As a Reader

★ Which words have the same or nearly the same meaning in each terse verse?

★ What rhyming words describe the fat-free hot dog and the clowning rabbit?

As a Writer

★ How is a terse verse like a joke or a pun?

★ Where do you think Kenneth got his ideas?

What would you call a rabbit who acts like a clown?

I'd say it's one funny bunny.

Terse Verse

Two rhyming words sum up the subject.

Make a Plan

Let the fun begin! Brainstorm some ideas for humorous writing of your own. Think of everyday events, such as riding the school bus, eating meals, or food shopping.

- List the events that remind you of funny situations.
- Pick three events and write them in a chart like the one below.
- Next to each event, write down whatever rhyming words and homonyms come to mind when you think of that event.

Event	Rhyming Words	Homonyms
1.		
2.		
3.		

Write It Down

Whether you write a joke, pun, or terse verse, try to make it funny. Use your chart for ideas.

- Include a punch line or an answer in a joke.
- In puns, use homonyms, or words that have the same pronunciation but different meanings.
- Use rhyming words to describe the subject of a terse verse. Rhyming dictionaries can give you more rhyming words to choose from.

Conferencing

Read what you have written to a partner. Does your partner think it's funny? Discuss words or details that could make your writing funnier.

Look It Over

Read your work to see if you are satisfied. Can you use assonance or consonance in your terse verse or puns? (See page 235.) Do questions end with question marks? Is dialogue set off in quotation marks? Fix any misspellings you find.

A Portrait in Words

Who's your biggest hero? Is it someone in sports or your community, or is it someone you know personally? People often like to learn about a person whose life and accomplishments they admire. Writers enjoy telling their readers about people they admire. When you write a true account of someone's life, it is called a **biography**.

A Biography
* ★ Presents facts about one person's life
* ★ Is told from the third-person point of view
* ★ Has a beginning, a middle, and an end
  <u>Beginning</u>: Introduces the person and tells why she or he is memorable
  <u>Middle</u>: Tells in detail one part of the person's life
  <u>End</u>: Tells what the writer thinks about this person
* ★ Tells about events in the order in which they happened
* ★ Uses vivid words to appeal to the senses
* ★ Includes details and stories to keep readers interested

Meet the Writer

Harriet Tubman had enormous courage. I wrote a biography to tell people about this amazing woman.

Brittany Presson
Tennessee

Think It Through

The subject of your biography should be someone you admire and find interesting. Look for ideas in your journal and log. Next, gather information about your subject. Then, think through what you want to say about the person.

Brainstorming

How do you find a person to write about? Try thinking about school subjects and people's achievements that interest you. Ask yourself what people you might enjoy learning about.

> Make a chart like Brittany's. Use the same subjects or choose others that interest you more. In each column, write the names of people that you admire.

Your Turn

Brittany's Chart			
History	Science	Sports	Music
Harriet Tubman	Albert Einstein	Teresa Weatherspoon	Backstreet Boys
John F. Kennedy	Rachel Carson		Wynton Marsalis
John Glenn	Bill Gates	Tiger Woods	Celine Dion

Select a Topic

Now, pick the three people you find the most interesting. Write a brief note about why each person is important.

Brittany's List		
History	Science	Sports
Harriet Tubman—helped slaves escape on the Underground Railroad	Rachel Carson—famous woman in ecology	Tiger Woods—youngest golfer to win Masters Tournament

Review your list to select the person you will write about.

- Which person's life interests you the most?
- Which would interest other people you know?
- Can you find information on this person?

Gather Information

Brittany selected Harriet Tubman for her subject and then gathered the facts and details she needed. The kinds of resources that she used to gather her information included books, magazines, CD-ROMs, the Internet, school texts, interviews, and the school librarian.

Portfolio

Don't lose your notes! Store them in your portfolio after each fact-gathering session.

Now, gather the information you need to write about your subject.

- Write your notes on index cards, one note to a card.
- At the top of each card, write the source of the information and include a page reference.
- If you are copying a quotation, use quotation marks and copy the exact words printed in your resource.

Here's a note Brittany wrote.

Harriet Tubman: Antislavery Activist, page 52

"By 1854, the woman called Moses was well known throughout the Eastern Shore, a legend among the slaves and a demon to the slaveholders."

Writer's Tip

Remember: If you think you need more facts and information, you can always go back and do more research.

Tech Tip

If your word processor has an Outline feature, use it to help you organize your notes.

Organize Information and Design a Plan

Brittany's next step was to organize her note cards. Brittany chose the most important and interesting facts. She arranged the cards in the order in which the events happened.

She identified the three main ideas from her note cards and then made an outline. She labeled her main ideas with Roman numerals and identified her supporting details with capital letters. See Brittany's outline on page 58.

Use Roman numerals to label main ideas. ••••••→

Use capital letters to identify details and supporting ideas. ••••

The first word begins with a capital letter. ••••

Each main idea becomes a paragraph. ••••

I. Introduce Harriet Tubman
  A. Born in Maryland in 1820 on a plantation
  B. Parents were slaves and poor
  C. Becomes famous because she helped slaves escape through the underground railroad

II. Harriet and the underground railroad
  A. Harriet escapes in 1849
  B. People in the underground railroad help her get to Philadelphia, Pennsylvania
  C. Stays there a year, and then makes 19 more trips to save other slaves
  D. Gets the nickname "Moses"
  E. Never captured, though there is a big reward

III. What I think about Harriet Tubman
  A. She freed many people and helped end slavery
  B. Her courage shows how important freedom is

Now, you're ready to organize your notes and make a plan.

- Choose the note cards with the most important and interesting information.
- Arrange the cards so that events are in the order in which they happened.
- Then, arrange the cards into groups of main ideas and supporting details.
- Make your outline. For help, see pages 267 and 269 in the *Writer's Handbook* section.

Remember to think about these things.

- Why is this person important?
- What event in this person's life is most important?
- What interesting details can I include?

Conferencing

Share your plan with a partner or partners. Do you have enough details to write an interesting biography? Keep focused and take notes as you listen to your partner's suggestions. Revise your plan to make it better.

Portfolio

Keep your plan in your portfolio and use it as a guide when you write your first draft.

Put It Into Words

Brittany wanted to get down on paper the most important and interesting facts about her subject. She reviewed her information, and then she wrote and wrote. Here is the first page of Brittany's draft. How well did she follow her outline?

Harriet Tubman
by Brittany Presson

Harriet Tubman's beginnings were very poor. She was born a slave in Bucktown, Maryland, in 1820. Her parents were slaves and they lived on a plantation. Despite this, Harriet became important in American history because of the underground railroad.

In 1849, Harriet heard that she was going to be sent south. She decided to escape, but before she ran off, she sung I'm bound for the Promised Land. It was up north, where slavery was not allowed. She would be free there.

That night she ran away through the woods and escaped to a house where she found people who helped her. That was how the underground railroad worked. They sent her to another house, where she was sent to another house and another house. She was able to avoid being captured because she knew how to find good hideing places outdoors. She finally reached freedom in Philadelphia, Pennsylvania.

A year later, Harriet decided to return to Maryland so that she could help other slaves escape. She made ninteen more trips in all, some with escape routes going all the way to Canada.

The beginning introduces the person and tells why she is important.

The writer uses the third-person point of view to tell the story.

The middle gives facts about one important part of the person's life.

Events are presented in the order in which they occurred.

Here's the rest of Brittany's biography. The last part is her conclusion, where she sums up her thoughts about Harriet Tubman.

The end summarizes what the writer thinks about this person.

Harriet had lots of cleverness, courage, and determination. In the end, she brought over 300 slaves to freedom. Everybody called her "Moses" because she led people out of slavery. There was a big reward for anyone who captured her, but no one ever did.

Harriet Tubman died on March 10, 1913, in Auburn, NY, when she was 93 years old. During her life she helped to free many people and to bring an end to slavery. Her courage has made many people, including me, know how important freedom is.

As you write your first draft, ask yourself

★ **Subject:**   Who is my subject?

★ **Audience:**   Who is my audience?

★ **Purpose:**   What is my goal?

★ **Form:**   What are the characteristics of a biography?

Now you are set to write the first draft of your biography. Use your note cards and outline. Remember, you will be able to make changes and add details later. For now, just focus on getting your thoughts on paper. This Drafting Checklist will help you.

Drafting Checklist

- The biography is written from the third-person point of view. You are the narrator.
- Many interesting facts are included.
- Events are presented in order.
- The story has a beginning, middle, and end.
  The **beginning** introduces the person and tells why he or she is memorable.
  The **middle** gives many facts about one part of the person's life.
  The **end** summarizes why you think this person is important.
- The biography has a title that grabs the reader's interest.

Conferencing

Read your draft to a partner. Does your partner think you included enough facts and details? Is there information that is not needed?

Take Another Look

Brittany had included many interesting facts about Harriet Tubman in her first draft. Still, she thought there were some ideas that weren't clear and some details that were missing. How do her revisions improve her biography?

Revise the title to make it more interesting for the reader. ·····►

Add a detail to clarify information. ·····►

Change sentence to make meaning clearer. ·►

Move sentence to where it makes more sense. ·►

Vary sentence length to make writing more interesting. ·····►

Harriet Tubman : Moses From the South
by Brittany Presson ∧

Harriet Tubman's beginnings were very poor. She was born a slave in Bucktown, Maryland, in 1820. Her parents were slaves and they lived on a plantation. Despite this, Harriet became important in American history because of the underground railroad.

to work for another slave owner
In 1849, Harriet heard that she was going to be sent south. She decided to escape, but before she ran off, she sung, I'm bound for
That land
the Promised Land. It was up north, where slavery was not allowed. She would be free there.

That night she ran away through the woods and escaped to a house where she found people who helped her. That was how the underground railroad worked. They sent her to another house, where she was sent to another house and another house. She was able to avoid being captured because she knew how to find good hideing places outdoors. She finally reached freedom in Philadelphia, Pennsylvania.

A year later, Harriet decided to return to Maryland so that she could help other slaves escape. She made ninteen more trips
had
in all, some with escape routes going all the way to Canada.

Now it's your chance to improve your writing. Read your first draft and decide what you like about it. What would you like to change?

Mark your revisions on your draft. Cross out words, add details, and jot down notes in the margin. Go back and find more information in your notes or do more research if you need to. Use the Revising Checklist to guide you.

Revising Marks

≡   capitalize
∧   add
⁊   remove
⊙   add a period
／   make lowercase
◯   move
∼   transpose

Revising Checklist

- Are the events presented in order?
- Is the third-person point of view used throughout your biography?
- Are there enough varied details to keep the reader interested?
- Are vivid words and precise words used?
- Do sentences vary in length and in how they begin?
- Can you add dialogue or a quotation to let your character speak for himself or herself?

Tech Tip

The Cut and Paste tools in your word-processing program can help you move words and sentences around.

Conferencing

Read your biography to your partner. Then, discuss the questions on the Revising Checklist. If your partner thinks that the answer to any question is "no," listen to his or her suggestions, and then decide what changes to make.

Portfolio

Save your revisions. When you edit and proofread your writing, you will need these changes.

Become a Super Writer

To keep your reader's interest, give details about the subject's life. For help, see the *Writer's Handbook* section, pages 223 and 233.

Polish Your Writing

Everyone makes mistakes or overlooks small errors when they write. That is why writers edit and proofread their work. What grammar, capitalization, punctuation, and spelling mistakes did Brittany find and correct?

Harriet Tubman: Moses From the South
by Brittany Presson

Add a comma in a compound sentence.

Capitalize a proper noun.

Put quotation marks around the words from a song.

Use the correct past-tense form of an irregular verb.

Correct a spelling mistake.

Capitalize a proper noun.

Harriet Tubman's beginnings were very poor. She was born a slave in Bucktown, Maryland, in 1820. Her parents were slaves ^,and they lived on a plantation. Despite this, Harriet became important in American history because of the underground railroad.

In 1849, Harriet heard that she was going to be sent south to work for another slave owner. She decided to escape, but before she ran off, she sung, "I'm bound for the Promised Land. That land was up north, where slavery was not allowed. She would be free there.

That night she ran away through the woods and escaped to a house where she found people who helped her. They sent her to another house, where she was sent to another house and another house. She was able to avoid being captured because she knew how to find good hideing places outdoors. That was how the underground railroad worked. She finally reached freedom in Philadelphia, Pennsylvania.

Now it's time to edit and proofread your biography for grammar, usage, spelling, and mechanics mistakes. Find a colored pencil and make your corrections. Use proofreading marks to show the changes. The Editing and Proofreading Checklist will help you get started.

Proofreading Marks

Mark	Meaning
¶	indent first line of paragraph
≡	capitalize
∧ or ∨	add
✗	remove
⊙	add a period
/	make lowercase
◯	spelling mistake
∽	move
∼	transpose

Editing and Proofreading Checklist

- Did I use all the parts of speech correctly?
  See the *Writer's Handbook* section, pages 248–264.
- Did I use a comma correctly in a compound sentence?
  See the *Writer's Handbook* section, page 271.
- Did I capitalize proper nouns and adjectives?
  See the *Writer's Handbook* section, page 266.
- Did I indent each paragraph?
  See the *Writer's Handbook* section, page 269.
- Did I spell all words correctly?
  See the *Writer's Handbook* section, pages 275–284.

Conferencing

Ask a classmate to read your biography. Can your classmate find any mistakes that you've missed? Talk about any errors he or she discovers. Add these corrections to your draft.

Tech Tip

A Spelling tool can't tell the difference between words such as *wear* and *where*. Carefully check all your words.

Portfolio

Keep your notes, outline, and drafts in your folder until you are ready to publish your work.

Become a Super Writer

Do you find yourself always using short sentences? Make compound sentences by combining two related sentences. For help, see the *Writer's Handbook* section, pages 244 and 246.

Share Your Work

Brittany felt that her writing captured who Harriet Tubman was and what was admirable about this Moses from the South. Read Brittany's final copy and decide for yourself.

Harriet Tubman: Moses From the South
by Brittany Presson

Harriet Tubman's beginnings were very poor. She was born a slave in Bucktown, Maryland, in 1820. Her parents were slaves, and they lived on a plantation. Despite this, Harriet became important in American history because of the Underground Railroad.

In 1849, Harriet heard that she was going to be sent south to work for another slave owner. She decided to escape, but before she ran off, she sang "I'm bound for the Promised Land." That land was up north, where slavery was not allowed. She would be free there.

That night she ran away through the woods and escaped to a house where she found people who helped her. They sent her to another house, where she was sent to another house and another house. She was able to avoid being captured because she knew how to find good hiding places outdoors. That was how the Underground Railroad worked. She finally reached freedom in Philadelphia, Pennsylvania.

A year later, Harriet decided to return to Maryland so that she could help other slaves escape. She made nineteen more trips in all. Some had escape routes going all the way to Canada. Harriet had lots of cleverness, courage, and determination. In the end, she brought over 300 slaves to freedom. Everybody called her "Moses" because she led people out of slavery just like the real Moses in the Bible. There was a big reward for anyone who captured her, but no one ever did.

Harriet Tubman died on March 10, 1913, in Auburn, NY, when she was 93 years old. She struggled to free many people and to bring an end to slavery. Her courage has made many people, including me, know how important freedom is.

Now it's your turn to share your work with your classmates. Here are some suggestions for publishing the biography you wrote. Choose one!

Act It Out ▶

Present a dramatic reading.

- Practice reading your work out loud in front of a mirror.
- Then, ask a friend to listen and to offer you helpful pointers.
- Before you present your reading, briefly explain why you chose the person. After reading, answer any questions your classmates may have.

◀ Book It

Publish your biography in a book along with other biographies your classmates wrote.

- Together think of a title and a design for your class's book.
- Include illustrations and photographs and discuss the best way to print and distribute it to your readers.

Poster Time ▶

Create a poster about your person.

- Place the biography in the center of a large piece of posterboard.
- Then, surround it with photos and illustrations that highlight the person's life. Display your poster in the classroom or ask your teacher if an exhibition spot in the school library or main display case can be arranged.

Writing a Mystery

Do you like mysteries? If you're like most people, you probably enjoy trying to solve a good "whodunit." In a **mystery,** there is a puzzling event or experience and a main character who tries to solve it. The writer gives clues that keep the reader wondering what will happen next. Only at the end of the story is the mystery solved.

The story you are about to read is an example of a mystery. The writer created a realistic experience and a story that keeps the reader guessing until the very end.

The setting and characters are realistic.

A puzzling event can't be explained.

Details keep the reader involved.

Dialogue keeps the reader interested.

Who's Following Me?

One dark night, a little boy had stayed in the park too long. It was late, and his mother was going to be mad. It was dark and it was a long, long way to his house. He started walking slowly out of the park.

The boy walked along slowly. Each time he took a step, he heard something behind him take a step, walking slowly along. He stopped and looked back. There was no one there. "Who's following me?" he said.

He walked a little faster. Each time he heard his shoe hit the sidewalk, he heard something else make a sound, like someone behind him taking a step—walking a little faster. He stopped and looked back. There was no one there. "Who's following me?" he said.

He started to run just a little. Each time his foot hit the ground, he heard something else, like feet behind him hitting the ground—starting to run just a little. He stopped and looked back. There was no one there . . . that he could see.

Talk About the Model

As a Reader

★ What did you learn about describing the setting?

★ How do you think the main character felt at the end of the story?

As a Writer

★ How does the writer pull the reader into the story?

★ How does the writer keep the reader interested?

★ How does the writer set up the reader for the surprise at the end?

He started to run fast. Each step he took, he heard someone behind him taking a step—starting to run fast. He didn't stop. He didn't look back. He ran and he ran and he ran.

He ran to his block and he ran to his yard and he ran to his porch. On the porch he stopped and looked back. There was no one there. But when he took another step he heard that noise again. He looked down at his shoe.

The sole was coming off his old shoe, and every time he took a step, the loose sole flapped and made a noise. He had been running from himself.

The character's fear is expressed.

Foreshadowing and pacing build suspense.

The puzzle is solved.

Make a Plan

To develop a plan for your mystery, you must think about your characters, the setting, and the puzzling event the main character will face.

Get to Know Your Characters and Setting

Choose characters for your story, and then explore who they are and what the setting is like.

- Begin by doing a quick write about your main character. Describe how your character looks and acts. Include his or her likes and dislikes. Your character should seem like a real person. Describe the other characters, too.

- Create a realistic setting for your mystery that is interesting and unusual. Would you see your character at home, in the woods, or at a shopping mall?

Choose What Happens to Your Character

Decide what puzzling event or experience will take place in your story. What mystery does your main character solve?

- Is something important missing?

- Is someone in danger?

- Has your character uncovered something mysterious?

Organize Your Writing

Use a story map to organize what happens in the beginning, middle, and end of your mystery.

CHARACTERS:	1. 2.	
SETTING:		Introduce the main characters, the setting, and the puzzling event.
PUZZLING EVENT:		
PLOT: Beginning	1. 2. 3.	Tell what happens: Give clues, details, and the characters' actions.
Middle	1. 2. 3. 4.	Solve the mystery and bring the story to a close.
End	1. 2.	

Write It Down

Jump Right In!

Start writing quickly. Follow your story map.

- To begin, introduce your main character and the setting or describe the puzzling event.
- Let the main character and the reader know that something very strange is happening or just about to happen.

Build the Suspense

Keep the reader wondering what will happen next.

- Give clues and add details.
- Describe how your main character reacts to the puzzling event and tries to solve it.
- Include dialogue to add interest.
- Use foreshadowing, suspense, and pacing to keep the reader glued to the page.

Solve the Mystery

Bring your story to a close.

- Show how your main character solves the mystery.
- Tie up all loose ends and answer any questions.
- Think of a title for your mystery and add it.

Conferencing

Read your mystery to a partner. Ask if your story was suspenseful. If not, what can be taken out so that the ending isn't given away, or what can be added to create more interest?

Tech Tip

Try out different words and ideas. If a sentence doesn't seem right, type new versions below it. Keep the one you like best.

Portfolio

Store your quick-write notes, story map, and draft. Later, you may decide you want to finish your mystery.

Look It Over

Reread your mystery to see if you want to make any changes. Could you add or take away details to make the mystery easier to solve or harder to solve?

If you decide to publish your mystery, be sure to revise it to make it as interesting and suspenseful as possible. Then, check that you haven't written any sentence fragments or run-ons. Carefully edit and proofread your story for grammar, spelling, punctuation, and capitalization.

Share Your Work

Talk to an Author

Your teacher might be able to arrange for your class to share its stories with a published author of children's mysteries. If possible, try to talk to the author in person or by video-conference. Find out what the author liked about your class's stories and what he or she might have done differently.

Publish Your Mystery in Print

Some publishers accept stories sent in by children for possible publication. Find out if your mystery might be just what they're looking for. Send your story (along with a self-addressed, stamped envelope) to

> *Stone Soup*
> c/o Editor
> P.O. Box 83
> Santa Cruz, CA 95063

> *Writing!*
> General Learning Communications
> 900 Skokie Boulevard, Suite 200
> Northbrook, IL 60062-4028

Publish Your Mystery on the Internet

Try publishing your story on the Internet. Send it to

KidPub (**http://www.kidpub.org/kidpub/**)
CyberKids (**http://www.cyberkids.com/**)

Travel to Zol

Can you imagine traveling to another planet or meeting an alien from a different galaxy? When you write a make-believe story that involves details about science and technology and probably takes place in the future, it is **science fiction**.

A Science-Fiction Story

★ Is usually set in the future

★ Refers frequently to science and technology

★ Has characters, a setting, and a plot that are interesting

★ Creates a conflict or a problem for the characters to solve

★ Is written with a beginning, a middle, and an end

★ Is suspenseful to keep readers interested

★ Concludes by telling how the characters solve the problem

Meet the Writer

I like anything to do with computers, rockets, and machines. I wrote this science-fiction story to tell a tale of problem-solving friends in outer space.

Simon Son
California

Think It Through

You really get to be creative when you write a science-fiction story. The setting, the characters, and the problem can all be as fantastic as you want.

Brainstorming

A good way to come up with story ideas is to think imaginatively and ask yourself questions like these.

- What characters will I use in the story? Which one will be the main character? What is he, she, or it like?

- What will happen in this story? Are my characters on a journey? Do certain events take place that set the stage for disaster, discovery, or success?

- Where and when does the story take place? Do the story's events occur on Earth or on some as yet unknown or unnamed planet? What is that place like? When in the future is the story set?

- What interesting titles can I think up for the story?

Think about the questions above. Then, make a chart like Simon's to record your story ideas.

Simon's Chart of Ideas

Characters	Problem	Setting	Title
Five good guys and a bad guy	Bad guy wants to stop the sun from shining.	City on planet Sharifa in a distant galaxy, in 2300	The Five Amazing Solvers
Superhero and a comet	A comet hits the planet.	Earth, in the year 2025	The Comet Disaster
Superhero and space monster	Space monster wants to gobble up the Milky Way.	The Milky Way 1,500 years from now	Space Monster's Revenge

Select a Topic

Look over your chart of possible story ideas. Decide which one you like the best. Use these questions to help you choose.

- Which would allow your imagination to soar?
- Which would let you create fantastic characters facing amazing problems?
- Which idea would your audience enjoy most?

Design a Plan

Simon selected "The Five Amazing Solvers" for his science-fiction story, and then he made a story map. Check his story map to see what he included in the beginning, middle, and end of his story. Where is the problem solved? What characters are involved? What is the setting like?

Title: The Five Amazing Solvers

Topic: A science-fiction adventure

BEGINNING

The characters, setting, and problem are introduced.

<u>Main Characters:</u> The five amazing solvers (Tico, Mito, Iko, Pico, Sipo) and Tarnished Medal

<u>Setting:</u> Zol, a city on the planet Sharifa, in the year 2300

<u>Problem:</u> A letter saying that the sun will stop shining on Zol

MIDDLE

Details about events in the plot are given.

1. The solvers identify the author of the letter.
2. The solvers travel to planet Gutto.
3. They confront Tarnished Medal.

END

The problem is solved, and the story concludes.

Tarnished Medal offers a bargain.

Finally, the problem is solved, and the amazing solvers return home safely.

Make a story map for your own science-fiction story. Organize it with a beginning, a middle, and an end. Think about these questions as you create your story map.

- Where and when does my story take place?
- Who are the main characters? What are they like?
- What is the problem the characters will face?
- What is the plot?
- How do the characters solve the problem?

Writer's Tip
As you map out your plot, keep your characters and setting in mind. This will help make your story's plot more believable.

Title:	
Topic:	
Beginning: Characters:	
Setting:	
Problem:	
Middle: Plot Events:	1.
	2.
	3.
	4.
End: Solution:	
Conclusion:	

Tech Tip
Use your word processor's Table tool to create a story map with rows and columns like the model shown.

Conferencing

Discuss your plan with a partner. Is the story set in the future? Does your partner understand the characters, setting, problem, and plot? What ideas or facts would make the plot clearer?

Portfolio

Keep your story map in your portfolio. Update your story map by adding new ideas or changes.

Put It Into Words

This is the first page of Simon's draft. As he wrote it, he didn't worry about making mistakes. He just kept writing. He couldn't wait to get his story on paper. What do you think about the problem Simon chose for his story?

The Five Amazing Solvers
by Simon Son

In a galaxy far, far away, on a planet named Sharifa in the year 2300, their lived five amazing people. What made them amazing was that they could solve problems that no one else could. Tico and Mito could both solve mysterys. Iko and Pico could read maps quickily. The leader, Sipo, was a good persuader, and he was the best solver of them all. The five solvers, as they called themselves, worked and stuck together when times got tough. They really stuck together when planet Sharifa got a strange letter. The letter said that the sun was never again going to shine over Zol, the capital city of Sharifa.

The amazing solvers went to work. Tico and Mito combined their powers and figured out that the meanest guy from planet Gutto had written the letter. Tico and Mito studied the handwriting and the post mark. They decided they better get to Gutto right away. Iko and Pico look at a map and led the solvers in a speedy flight to the planet.

The setting and characters are introduced.

The story is set in the future.

The problem is stated.

The plot is developed.

Technology is referred to.

Read the rest of Simon's story below. Do you think Simon followed his story map as he wrote? Do you like his story? Why or why not?

The solvers found Tarnished Medal just as he was about to fly into the sky and push the sun away. Sipo told him, "if you push

Conflict and suspense are used to build interest. ····▶ away the sun, no one will have any light, not even you. He also told Tarnished Medal that the sun was real hot it wouldn't be an easy trick to play.

Technology is referred to. ·········▶ Sipo's arguments made sense, but Tarnished Medal was proud. He knew his heat-resistant suit and reflective goggles would protect him.

To save face, Tarnished Medal bargained with the solvers.

The problem is resolved. ·········▶ The sun will shine on Zol so long as planet Gutto has water, Medal growled. The amazing solvers gave their oaths that this would be so and Tarnished Medal agreed to the bargain. All the solvers then flew home feeling like heros. When they landed safely back on Sharifa, Sipo cheered, "There will always be plenty of water on Gutto. The crisis is over."

Think Like a Writer

As you write your first draft, ask yourself

★ **Subject:** What is the conflict or problem?

★ **Audience:** Who are my readers?

★ **Purpose:** What is my goal?

★ **Form:** What are the characteristics of a science-fiction story?

You have a good plan, so now you are ready to write your first draft. Review your story's setting, characters, problem, and plot. Then, follow your story map as you write. If you leave out anything or make mistakes, you can make corrections later. Use the Drafting Checklist as a guide.

Drafting Checklist

- The story is set in the future.
- Interesting characters are used.
- The characters are faced with a conflict or problem.
- The story has a beginning, middle, and end.
- The story refers to science or technology to make the details and events seem real.
- The story keeps readers in suspense.
- The conflict or problem is solved at the end of the story.

When you have finished your first draft, reconsider your title. Is it catchy enough? If not, brainstorm new titles. Pick the one that will capture the interest of your readers.

Conferencing

Work with a partner on your first draft. Ask if your story is suspenseful. Is the plot believable, and does it make sense? Are there any details that need to be explained more?

Revising Take Another Look

When Simon reread his first draft, he liked most of what he had written. He made some revisions, though, to improve his story. Here is the first page of his revised draft. What do you think of the changes he made?

The Five Amazing Solvers
by Simon Son

In a galaxy far, far away, on a planet named Sharifa in the year 2300, their lived five amazing people. What made them amazing was that they could solve problems that no one else

Replace words with better ones. ⟶ could. Tico and Mito could both solve mysterys. Iko and Pico
could change peoples minds
could read maps quickily. The leader, Sipo, ~~was a good~~
persuader, and he was the best solver of them all. The five

solvers, as they called themselves, worked and stuck together

Revise to add suspense and describe problem better. ⟶ when times got tough. They really stuck together when planet
Sharifa got a strange letter. The letter said that the sun was
Nobody had signed the letter.
never again going to shine over Zol, the capital city of Sharifa.

Add detail to clarify the writing. ⟶ The amazing solvers went to work. Tico and Mito combined
They   in the galaxy, Tarnished Medal,
their powers and figured out that the meanest guy from planet

Rewrite a confusing section to improve the order of ideas. ⟶ Gutto had written the letter. ~~Tico and Mito~~ studied the
handwriting and the post mark. They decided they better get to

Gutto right away. Iko and Pico look at a map and led the

solvers in a speedy flight to the planet.

Here are more of Simon's revisions. What other revisions do you think Simon could have made to improve his story?

at the Gutto Launchpad,
The solvers found Tarnished Medal just as he was about to fly ◄···· **Add detail to clarify writing.**

into the sky and push the sun away. Sipo told him, "if you push

away the sun, no one will have any light, not even you. He also

told Tarnished Medal that the sun was real hot it wouldn't be an

easy trick to play.

Sipo's arguments made sense, but Tarnished Medal was

proud. He knew his heat-resistant suit and reflective goggles
Suddenly, though, his mind raced back to last ◄ **Add flashback to tell about something that happened at an earlier time.**
year's Festival of the Planets, and he saw his
would protect him. children playing by the lake on Gutto. Maybe
he really shouldn't push the sun away.
To save face, Tarnished Medal bargained with the solvers.

The sun will shine on Zol so long as planet Gutto has water,

Add detail to explain something.

Medal growled. The amazing solvers gave their oaths that this

would be so and Tarnished Medal agreed to the bargain. All the

solvers then flew home feeling like heros. When they landed

safely back on Sharifa, Sipo cheered, "There will always be
because we control the water
plenty of water on Gutto. The crisis is over."

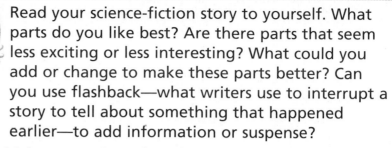

Revising Marks

≡ capitalize

∧ add

✗ remove

⊙ add a period

/ make lowercase

⌒ move

∾ transpose

Read your science-fiction story to yourself. What parts do you like best? Are there parts that seem less exciting or less interesting? What could you add or change to make these parts better? Can you use flashback—what writers use to interrupt a story to tell about something that happened earlier—to add information or suspense?

Make corrections directly on your draft. Remember, you may need to revise your writing more than once. Use the Revising Checklist to help you decide what changes to make.

Revising Checklist

- Does your story have a definite beginning, middle, and end?
- Are there enough details to keep your readers interested?
- Is it clear what the problem is?
- Did you use flashback to give facts about important things that happened earlier?
- Is your story suspenseful?

Tech Tip

Store older versions of your draft on your hard drive or disk. That way you can go back to an earlier version if you want to.

Portfolio

Store your revised work until you are ready to edit and proofread it.

Conferencing

Read your science-fiction story to a partner. Have your partner answer the Revising Checklist questions. Talk about ways to improve your story. Listen to your partner's suggestions and take notes to remember them.

Become a Super Writer

To give your readers enough details and interesting facts, use flashback. For help, see the *Writer's Handbook* section, page 225.

Polish Your Writing

Simon reread his revisions and thought his story had turned out OK. Now, he just had to edit and proofread his writing to fix his grammar, spelling, and punctuation mistakes. What mistakes did he correct? Are there any mistakes that he missed?

The Five Amazing Solvers
by Simon Son

In a galaxy far, far away, on a planet named Sharifa in the
                    there
year 2300, ~~their~~ lived five amazing people. What made them

amazing was that they could solve problems that no one else
                                    mysteries
could. Tico and Mito could both solve ~~mysterys~~ Iko and Pico
                quickly
could read maps ~~quickily.~~ The leader, Sipo, could change peoples'

minds, and he was the best solver of them all. The five

solvers, as they called themselves, worked and stuck together

when times got tough. They really stuck together when planet

Sharifa got a strange letter. The letter said that the sun was

never again going to shine over Zol, the capital city of Sharifa.

Nobody had signed the letter.

The amazing solvers went to work. Tico and Mito combined
                                        postmark
their powers and studied the handwriting and the ~~post mark.~~

They figured out that the meanest guy in the galaxy,

Tarnished Medal, from planet Gutto, had written the letter.

They decided they better get to Gutto right away.

Spell the homonym *there* correctly.

Form the plural noun correctly.

Spell a word with the suffix *ly* correctly.

Add an apostrophe to show possession.

Form the compound word *postmark* correctly.

Here are more of Simon's corrections. Why do you think he worked so hard to get his story just right?

Change the verb to past tense to match other verbs.

looked
Iko and Pico ~~look~~ at a map and led the solvers in a speedy flight to the planet.

The solvers found Tarnished Medal at the Gutto Launchpad, just as he was about to fly into the sky and push the sun away.

Capitalize the first word in dialogue.

Add a quotation mark after the speaker's words.

Sipo told him, "if you push away the sun, no one will have any light, not even you. He also told Tarnished Medal that the sun

very   , so
was ~~real~~ hot it wouldn't be an easy trick to play.

Correct a problem word.

Fix a run-on sentence.

Sipo's arguments made sense, but Tarnished Medal was proud. He knew his heat-resistant suit and reflective goggles would protect him. Suddenly, though, his mind raced back to last year's Festival of the Planets, and he saw his children playing by the lake on Gutto. Maybe he really shouldn't push the sun away.

To save face, Tarnished Medal bargained with the solvers.

Put a quotation mark before and after the speaker's words.

The sun will shine on Zol so long as planet Gutto has water, Medal growled. The amazing solvers gave their oaths that this

Put a comma in a compound sentence.

would be so and Tarnished Medal agreed to the bargain. All

heroes
the solvers then flew home feeling like (heros). When they landed

Spell an irregular plural noun correctly.

safely back on Sharifa, Sipo cheered, "There will always be plenty of water on Gutto because we control the water.

Use an exclamation point to show strong emotion.

!
The crisis is over.

It's time now for you to edit and proofread your science-fiction story. Check your grammar, usage, spelling, and mechanics. Use a colored pencil and proofreading marks to show your corrections. The Editing and Proofreading Checklist can help guide you.

Proofreading Marks

Mark	Meaning
⌐	indent first line of paragraph
≡	capitalize
∧ or ∨	add
ℒ	remove
⊙	add a period
/	make lowercase
⟋	spelling mistake
⟲	move
∿	transpose

Editing and Proofreading Checklist

- Are the plurals of irregular nouns formed correctly?
  See the *Writer's Handbook* section, page 249.
- Are apostrophes that show possession used correctly?
  See the *Writer's Handbook* section, page 272.
- Did I use quotation marks to show dialogue?
  See the *Writer's Handbook* section, page 273.
- Did I spell homonyms and other problem words correctly?
  See the *Writer's Handbook* section, page 283.
- Did I spell all words correctly?
  See the *Writer's Handbook* section, pages 275–284.
- Is my handwriting neat and easy to read?
  See the *Writer's Handbook* section, page 274.

Tech Tip
The same key is used for quotation marks and apostrophes. Press that key and the Shift key together for quotation marks.

Portfolio
Organize and label everything. That way you can find your final copy easily when you are ready to publish it.

Conferencing

Share your story with a partner. Can your partner find any mistakes that you missed? If you're both unsure about a word's spelling, check the dictionary.

Become a Super Writer

Make sure you form the plurals of irregular nouns correctly. For help, see the *Writer's Handbook* section, page 249.

Share Your Work

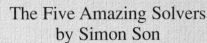

Here is the final version of Simon's science-fiction story. He decided to publish his story as an audio book. How do you think it turned out?

The Five Amazing Solvers
by Simon Son

In a galaxy far, far away, on a planet named Sharifa in the year 2300, there lived five amazing people. What made them amazing was that they could solve problems that no one else could. Tico and Mito could both solve mysteries. Iko and Pico could read maps quickly. The leader, Sipo, could change people's minds, and he was the best solver of them all. The five solvers, as they called themselves, worked and stuck together when times got tough. They really stuck together when planet Sharifa got a strange letter. The letter said that the sun was never again going to shine over Zol, the capital city of Sharifa. Nobody had signed the letter.

The amazing solvers went to work. Tico and Mito combined their powers and studied the handwriting and the postmark. They figured out that the meanest guy in the galaxy, Tarnished Medal, from planet Gutto, had written the letter. They decided they better get to Gutto right away. Iko and Pico looked at a map and led the solvers in a speedy flight to the planet.

The solvers found Tarnished Medal at the Gutto Launchpad, just as he was about to fly into the sky and push the sun away. Sipo told him, "If you push away the sun, no one will have any light, not even you." He also told Tarnished Medal that the sun was very hot, so it wouldn't be an easy trick to play.

Sipo's arguments made sense, but Tarnished Medal was proud. He knew his heat-resistant suit and reflective goggles would protect him. Suddenly, though, his mind raced back to last year's Festival of the Planets, and he saw his children playing by the lake on Gutto. Maybe he really shouldn't push the sun away.

To save face, Tarnished Medal bargained with the solvers. "The sun will shine on Zol so long as planet Gutto has water," Medal growled. The amazing solvers gave their oaths that this would be so, and Tarnished Medal agreed to the bargain. All the solvers then flew home feeling like heroes. When they landed safely back on Sharifa, Sipo cheered, "There will always be plenty of water on Gutto because we control the water. The crisis is over!"

You've put a lot of work into your story. Now it's time to share it. Choose one of the suggestions shown here or use one of your own.

Sci-Fi on Tape ▶

Make an audio book for your audience. Practice reading your science-fiction story aloud. Use lots of expression and try changing the sound of your voice for different characters. Include background music and sound effects, too. When you're ready, make a tape of your reading.

◀ Comic Book Heroes

Create a comic book based on your story. Draw action-packed scenes with bright, vivid colors and write speech balloons to make your science-fiction story into a real comic book. If you want, use the Create-A-Comic blank book to help you prepare your comic book.

Sci-Fi Festival ▶

Plan a Science-Fiction Festival with other students.

- Display your stories near a large movie-type poster that announces the date and time of the festival.
- During the event, take turns reading your stories aloud.
- Consider dramatizing one or more of the stories for your Science-Fiction Festival.

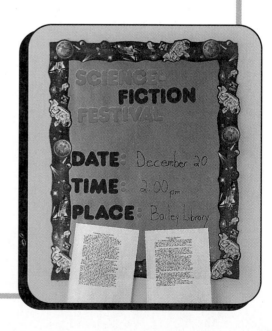

Writing a Myth

Do you know about the adventures of Hercules, the strongman of ancient Greece? What about the tales of Raven, the tricky bird from the Pacific Northwest? These imaginative stories are called **myths**. They explain things about nature, the origin of the world, or human experiences.

"The Origin of the Ox" comes from China. It takes place at some unknown time in the distant past. Although its main characters are a god and an animal, the writer presents a human problem and explains how the problem was solved.

Talk About the Model

As a Reader

★ What problem does the story describe? How does the problem get solved?

★ Why do you think the Emperor of Heaven wants the people to think well of him?

As a Writer

★ Why do you think the writer calls the Ox a stupid creature?

★ What message do you think the writer is telling with this story?

The setting is an earlier time.

The Origin of the Ox

Long ago, life was very hard—even harder than it is today. People had to struggle in the fields with their bare hands to grow enough food to feed themselves. They rarely had enough to eat—even though they worked day and night.

The Emperor of Heaven saw the poor people toiling on the earth and took pity on them. He summoned the Ox star from the sky and sent it down to tell the people that if they worked hard, they would be able to eat well every third day.

The Ox rushed down to pass on the news. But it was a stupid creature, and so proud of being the Emperor's messenger that it muddled the message. The Ox told the people that if they worked hard, the Emperor of Heaven said they could have three meals a day!

The Emperor of Heaven did not want the people on earth to think that he broke his promises, so the Ox found itself yoked to a plow to till the fields. People just couldn't have done all the work by themselves.

The writer uses vivid verbs, adverbs, and adjectives.

The characters and their problem are introduced.

The main characters are a god and an animal.

The end tells how the problem was solved and explains the origin of plowing fields with oxen.

Make a Plan

Before you begin writing, you'll need a plan. To make one, first, choose your characters and setting.

Get to Know Your Characters and Setting

The main characters in a myth can be humans, animals, and gods or goddesses.

- Choose the characters you want to use in your myth.
- Write a quick sketch describing each character and the role he or she will play.

Then, imagine a setting—another world at an earlier time—that suits your myth. Picture your characters being in this setting. Write a quick sketch to describe the setting.

Choose What Happens to Your Characters

State the main topic of your myth. It could be a problem to solve, or it could be an explanation of something in nature, how the world came to be, or a human behavior. For example, there are many myths that explain love, sickness, and even the weather.

Organize Your Writing

Design a plan for your myth. Use a chart to help you organize your writing. Introduce your characters and setting in the beginning. In the middle, describe the problem and what happens to your characters. End your myth by telling how the problem is solved and what happens to the characters.

Characters:			
Setting:			End
Problem:	Beginning	Middle	
Events:			

Write It Down

Once you have finished your plan, you can start to write your myth.

Choose a Way to Begin

- Start your myth by introducing your main characters and your setting. Choose either your characters or your setting to focus on first.

- Catch your readers' attention in the first couple of sentences. Use vivid words, idioms, or exaggeration. Maybe pose a question to involve your readers.

Keep Your Readers Interested

- Identify and describe the problem.

- Explain each character's role and what happens to that character. Are the characters part of the problem? Do they cause or solve the problem?

- Use personification for characters that are not people. *Personification* means "to give human qualities to something that is not a person."

- Use exaggeration to make some of your characters seem larger than life. This will entertain your readers.

Write a Believable Ending

- Tell how the problem is solved or explain why something takes place.

- Be sure to explain what happens to the main characters in your myth.

Conferencing

Read your myth to a partner. Ask whether your myth seems imaginative. Does it offer a good explanation or solution to the problem?

Look It Over

Reread your myth. Are there any changes you want to make? Are there sentences that can be combined or expanded to improve your writing? Have you entertained your readers? Don't forget, you can revise your writing again later. If you choose to publish your myth, be sure to edit and proofread it.

Tech Tip
Set your page for double spacing on your first draft and revisions. Use single spacing for your final copy.

Portfolio

Keep your chart, notes, drafts, and a floppy disk with copies of your drafts in case you decide to publish.

Writing a Play

Have you been in a play or skit? Acting can be great fun. It's also fun to write a **play**—a story in dialogue form that actors perform for an audience. It can be based on a real-life experience or a make-believe one.

What follows is part of *How to Eat Fried Worms*. The dialogue sounds realistic—the way people talk in real life. Actors know when to speak because their characters' names are in front of their speeches. Stage directions tell how the characters sound, act, or move.

The problem is introduced.

from **How to Eat Fried Worms**

ALAN: Yeah. You wouldn't really eat a worm. You say you would, but if you were sitting at the table, with a worm on your plate. . . . *(He gestures—a plate, the worm—makes a face.)* Glah! Geez!

BILLY: *(sitting up, holding out his hand to ALAN)* You want to bet? Come on. I'll bet you I can eat a worm.

ALAN: *(derisively)* Yeah. Come on.

BILLY: Whatta you mean, come on? You want to bet or not?

ALAN: *(biting his fingernail)* Yeah, well you might be able to eat one, but that's not the same as really eating worms. If Tom's mother'd said she'd give him fifty dollars if he'd eat a bite of the salmon, he'd have eaten it.

BILLY: Okay. So we'll make it three worms, one a day for three days. *(to TOM)* If I ate them all at once, I'd choke. *(He grabs his own neck, pretends to gag.)*

TOM: Geez.

ALAN: No. *(He gets up.)* No, it's gotta be fifteen worms. And I get to pick them, not just little tiny ones. . . .

Stage directions describe the character's actions.

There are at least two main characters.

Dialogue and actions show what the character is feeling.

JOE: Here it is. Looks good enough to eat.

(BILLY glops on ketchup, mustard, picks up the fork, hesitates, gazing at the plate, glops on piccalilli, peanut butter, picks up fork, puts it down, squeezes on some lemon juice, spoons on raspberry jam.) ◄ ······· The character's actions are realistic.

TOM: That's not going to do any good. Think fish: fish, fish, fish, fish.

(BILLY begins to eat, glancing now and then at ALAN and JOE, who are whispering in the corner. Then he puts down the fork and begins to spread on more condiments.)

TOM: Come on. You've got everything on already.

(BILLY looks at TOM, then holds the fork out to him.)

BILLY: You eat some if you're in such a hurry.

JOE: No, no. The bet was *you* were going to eat fifteen worms in fifteen days, not him and you together.

BILLY: All right *(eating the last bite)*, I'll go get another one for him. *(to TOM)* You're so big—*(he mimics)*—hurry up, what's a worm? Don't be a sissy—fish, fish, fish, fish.

◄ ······· The dialogue sounds natural.

JOE: *(taking a worm out of his shirt pocket)* Here, I brought an extra one today.

TOM: *(uncomfortably)* I didn't say sissy. I can't help it if my father told me to be home by two.

BILLY: *(wiping his mouth and standing up)* You got time.

TOM: *(edging back)* It's not even cooked.

ALAN: *(taking worm)* I'll cook it. *(He grabs up saucepan, starts to run out Center, falls down, clambers up, exits.)*

(A silence)

JOE: *(to TOM)* If you don't eat it, you're chicken—after all your talk.

TOM: No, see, my father . . . *(He scratches his elbow, glancing around.)*

BILLY: Three minutes aren't going to make any difference.

(BILLY starts putting the tops back on the bottles and jars. Suddenly TOM bolts out stage right.)

BILLY: *(running after him)* Get him!

> Stage directions are set in italics and within parentheses.

> The speaker's name is written in capital letters followed by a colon.

> The beginning of each character's dialogue is capitalized.

Talk About the Model

As a Reader
★ What do you think the setting is?
★ How would you describe the characters?
★ Do you think the story is real or made up? Why?

As a Writer
★ How does the writer tell what the problem is?
★ How are the characters brought to life?
★ How does the writer capture his audience's interest?

Make a Plan

Develop a plan for your play before you begin writing.

Identify Your Characters

Your play should have at least two main characters.

- Model your characters on people in real life.
- Begin by making notes about each character.
- Describe how your characters look, act, and speak.

Choose a Problem and Setting

Your play must have a problem that your characters solve and a setting.

- Think of a problem your characters can try to solve. All the events in your play will connect with this problem.
- Decide where you want the play to take place. Will every scene be set in the same place, or will the action take place in different locations?

Organize Your Writing

Your play can have just one scene or many scenes. Decide what will happen in each scene in your play. Use a chart like the one below to map out your plan for your play.

- Introduce the characters, problem, and setting. If you wish to include information about things that happened before the play started, this is the time to add it.
- Determine the main event in each scene. Note the characters in the scene and the setting, if it changes.
- Tell how the characters solve or don't solve their problem in the last scene or the end.

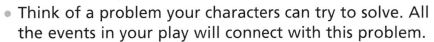

	Scene 1	Scene 2	Scene 3
Characters:			
Setting:			
Problem:			
What happens:			

Write It Down

Now write your play. Keep your notes and chart handy for ideas and to keep your play moving on track.

Start Off With a Bang!

- Introduce your main characters, the problem, and the setting.
- Use stage directions to tell the characters how to speak, act, and move.

Keep Your Audience Interested

- Use lots of dialogue to help your audience understand the characters and their connection with the problem.
- Show your characters' actions and reactions to what is happening in the story.
- Treat each main event as a separate scene.
- Follow the correct format for a play.
- Write the characters' names in all capital letters, followed by a colon, before their spoken words.
- Set stage directions in italics and within parentheses.

Get to the Final Curtain

- Wrap up what's happening to conclude your play.
- Have your characters resolved their problem? Would a surprise ending help?

Tech Tip

Set all the characters' names in uppercase type. Use italic type for any stage directions you include.

Conferencing

Have your partner help you test out your play. Assign roles and read your play aloud. Does your play sound realistic? Was it easy for your partner to follow? Are the stage directions clear?

Look It Over

Reread your play to see if you want to change anything. Can you add new events or change the dialogue or stage directions to improve your play? Remember, you can always go back and revise your play. If you go on to publish it, be sure to edit and proofread your writing.

Portfolio

Store your notes, chart, and drafts. Keep them handy if you decide to have your play performed.

IMAGINE THAT

Writing to Describe

Writing a Descriptive Paragraph

How does a hot summer day feel or freshly baked bread smell? In a **descriptive paragraph**, the writer uses vivid words to capture sights, sounds, feelings, tastes, and smells. Jimmy describes one experience during his summer vacation in "A Sunshine Kind of Day." His words and details create a clear picture of that experience.

Meet the Writer

My mom and I visit our relatives in Ohio every summer. To remember what the fun things my cousins and I do are like, I write about them.

Jimmy Garcia
California

A Sunshine Kind of Day
by Jimmy Garcia

Today was a great day! Ellie, Todd, and I had raced down to the creek. We huffed and puffed and were sweating a lot. The blazing sun made the air really hot and heavy. It was so hot beads of salty sweat formed a wet mustache on my face. When we stepped into the chilly water of the creek, we cooled off quickly. The small stones on the bottom felt like ice cubes. The stones had been polished smooth by the creek. Todd discovered one that had a fossil in it. The sunshine coming through the trees made patches of green and gold all around us. A kingfisher with bright blue feathers was fishing along the creek. We could hear his clackety call as he flew off and disappeared into the bright sky. It was really neat!

Talk About the Model

★ How does the writer let you know how he feels?

★ What vivid sensory words does the writer use
to make the description come to life?

Make a Plan

Choose a topic that you can describe in one paragraph.
The topic can be a person, an event, a place, or an idea.

- Write down the five senses.
- Next to each sense, list some details that will help your
  readers see, hear, taste, feel, and touch your topic.

Write It Down

Now write your descriptive paragraph.

- Start with a sentence that tells what your
  topic is or the scene you want to describe.
- Use words that create images readers
  can see, hear, touch, taste, and smell.
- Prepositions, such as *on, after, below,* and
  from, can help you describe the scene.
- Organize your description so it will be easy
  to follow. Use an order such as top to bottom,
  or most important to least important.

Tech Tip
**Put a header at
the top of every
page you write.
Include the type of
writing and the
number of the
draft.**

Conferencing

Read your descriptive paragraph aloud to a partner.
Do the sensory words you used make your subject
seem real? If not, what better ones can you use?

Look It Over

Before you publish your descriptive paragraph,
read it again. Where could you have used more
vivid words? Are all your ideas in a logical order?
Have you used prepositional phrases correctly?

Portfolio
Store your descriptive
paragraph. Use a large
paper clip to keep
together any notes
that you have
made.

Writing Poetry: Cinquain and Concrete Poem

Poetry comes in many shapes, sizes, and styles. Whatever type of poetry you choose to write, your goal is usually the same: Write what you want to say in the clearest, most vivid way possible.

Cinquain

Cinq (sank) is the French word for "five," and a **cinquain** (sing KAYN) is a five-line poem. Each line has a certain number of syllables. Line one usually has two syllables, line two has four, line three has six, line four has eight, and line five has two. Cinquains sometimes have rhyming words in them, but they don't have to.

This cinquain was written by Thomas D. Greer. It is part of a series of cinquains. Mr. Greer wrote it to share some of his feelings about being a father.

Meet the Writer

Thomas Greer is a computer programmer who enjoys music and writing poetry. His poems appear in books and in poetry workshops on the World Wide Web.

> Writing poetry is about being alert.... Pay attention, and write what you see.

Talk About the Model

As a Reader

★ What action does the poem describe?

★ Why do you think the children are so interested?

As a Writer

★ Why do you think the writer uses so many action words at the beginning of the poem?

★ How do you think the writer found words with the number of syllables he needed for each line?

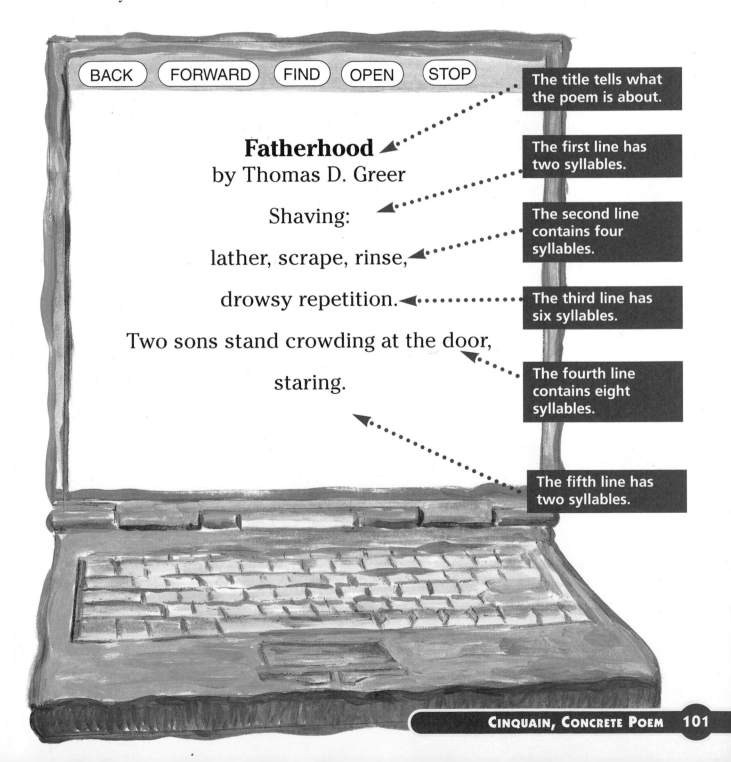

BACK   FORWARD   FIND   OPEN   STOP

Fatherhood
by Thomas D. Greer

Shaving:

lather, scrape, rinse,

drowsy repetition.

Two sons stand crowding at the door,

staring.

The title tells what the poem is about.

The first line has two syllables.

The second line contains four syllables.

The third line has six syllables.

The fourth line contains eight syllables.

The fifth line has two syllables.

Concrete Poem

A **concrete poem** is written in the shape of the object it describes. This one was written by Lillian Morrison. Like many of her poems, it grew out of her experiences as a child growing up in Jersey City, New Jersey.

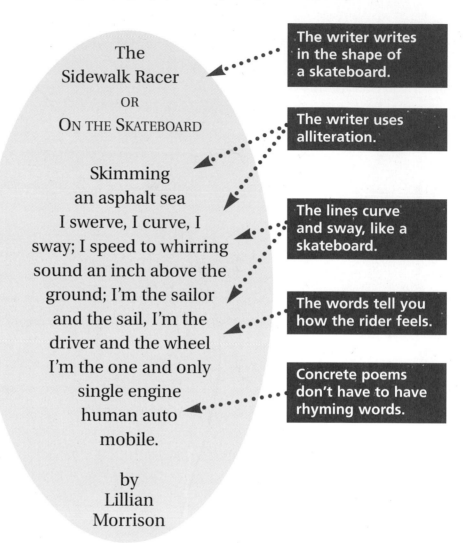

The
Sidewalk Racer
OR
ON THE SKATEBOARD

Skimming
an asphalt sea
I swerve, I curve, I
sway; I speed to whirring
sound an inch above the
ground; I'm the sailor
and the sail, I'm the
driver and the wheel
I'm the one and only
single engine
human auto
mobile.

by
Lillian
Morrison

The writer writes in the shape of a skateboard.

The writer uses alliteration.

The lines curve and sway, like a skateboard.

The words tell you how the rider feels.

Concrete poems don't have to have rhyming words.

Talk About the Model

As a Reader

★ Does the shape of the poem relate to its topic?

★ How does the poem make you feel about it?

★ What words in the poem bring the action to life?

As a Writer

★ How does the writer let you know what the poem is about?

★ Why do you think the writer chose to have some rhyming words and alliteration in the poem?

Make a Plan

Decide whether you would like to write a cinquain or a concrete poem—or both! Then, start planning.

Choose a Topic

- Brainstorm ideas for topics.
- Make a list of possible topics.
- Select a topic for your poem.

Gather Ideas

Use a cluster to organize your thoughts. Write your topic in the middle, and then let the ideas flow.

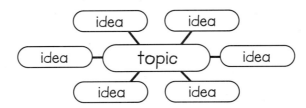

Organize Your Writing

Use the form of the poem to organize it.

- If you are writing a concrete poem, draw the shape of your topic on the paper.
- If you are writing a cinquain, make a form with blanks for the number of syllables in each line.

Write It Down

Let's Get Started

- If you are writing a concrete poem, start to fill the poem's shape with your title or other beginning words.
- If you're writing a cinquain, choose words and write them down. Follow the organizer so you will have the right number of syllables in each line.
- Use sensory words in your poem.

Keep Going . . .

- Consider adding some rhyming words to your cinquain or concrete poem. These can be pleasing to the ear.
- To add interest, use onomatopoeia—words that sound like the things they refer to, such as *swoosh* or *fizz.*
- Writing several words that begin with the same sound, like *spinning sparkling spaceship,* creates the interesting effect called alliteration.
- If your concrete poem is about something that moves, such as a locomotive, try adding words that create rhythm in the poem.

The Finish Line

- Think of a title for your cinquain and write it above the poem.
- If you didn't include the title in your concrete poem, think of one to add now.

Tech Tip
Use the Format buttons to center lines or make them line up on the left or the right.

Conferencing

Read your poem to your partner. Does your partner think you followed the form correctly? Do the images make the subject come alive?

Portfolio

Keep your notes, organizers, and drafts. You'll want to look at them each time you revise your poem.

Look It Over

Reread your poem. Are there words that you can add, move, or delete? Are all the words spelled correctly? If you wrote a cinquain, does it have enough syllables? Make changes until your poem feels right to you.

Like a Diamond in the Sky

What is "like a diamond in the sky"? According to the old nursery rhyme "Twinkle, Twinkle, Little Star," it's a star. There are many kinds of diamonds, though. One kind is a poem. It's called a **diamante.** It has seven lines, and it is shaped like a diamond.

A Diamante

* Begins and ends with nouns that have opposite meanings
* Has a diamond shape
* Follows special rules for each of its seven lines (see page 107)
* Uses vivid words
* Can have literal words that are used for exact meaning or figurative words that are used in imaginative ways

Meet the Writer

Last summer, my family and I went camping out west. The mountains there are very different from the soft, round mountains of Virginia, where I live.

Glen Fry
Virginia

Think It Through

The first step in writing a diamante is to choose two nouns. The nouns should name two opposite things, places, or people that you find interesting.

Brainstorming

Think about lots of different nouns. You may want to read through your journal or log or look around your school or community for ideas.

Write down nouns that really interest you. They can be places, things, or people. Next, think of their opposites. One word may trigger another . . . and another . . . and another. Make a list as long as you can, and then take a look at Glen's list.

Glen's List

town ←→ city

water ←→ land

rain ←→ sunshine

mountain ←→ valley

dog ←→ cat

teacher ←→ student

Select a Topic

Look at your list.

- Which combination of nouns interests you the most?
- Which nouns are really opposites of each other?
- Choose the most interesting pair of nouns to use for your diamante.

Design a Plan

A diamante has exact rules that can give you your plan. Glen used the rules to organize his ideas for his topic of mountain and valley. Notice how he wrote his words beneath the rules. He also wrote several ideas for lines 2–6.

Rules for a Diamante

Line 1: One noun that is the opposite of the noun in line 7
<u>mountain</u>

Line 2: Two adjectives that describe the word in line 1
<u>big, huge, gigantic, humongous, monstrous</u>

Line 3: Three words ending in *ing* or *ed* that tell about the word in line 1
<u>towering, jagged, rugged, peaked, sloping</u>

Line 4: Two words about the word in line 1 and two words about the word in line 7
<u>tall, high, hill, U-shaped, glen, lowland</u>

Line 5: Three words ending in *ing* or *ed* that tell about the word in line 7
<u>lying, farming, hollowed, plowed, flattened</u>

Line 6: Two adjectives that describe the word in line 7
<u>low, deep, gentle, grassy, green, peaceful</u>

Line 7: One noun that is the opposite of the noun in line 1
<u>valley</u>

Your Turn

Now, organize your ideas.

- Create a rules form like the one Glen used.
- Write your two nouns on the first and last lines.
- Then, add vivid words on the other lines until you have lots of words to choose from.
- Include figurative words—words that are not used for their exact meaning but for their imaginative meanings—if you like.

Conferencing

Share your plan with a partner or partners. Listen and take notes about their suggestions.

Portfolio

Save your plan and use it when you write your first draft.

Put It Into Words

A first draft is a creative stage of writing. It's not perfect, it's not finished. It really shouldn't be any of those things. It's just all your ideas written down for the first time.

Here is Glen's first draft. What does it make you think of?

The writer uses two vivid adjectives about the noun in line 1.

Words ending in *ing* and *ed* are used for the noun in line 1.

The writer includes two words about the noun in line 1 and two words about the noun in line 7.

Words ending in *ing* and *ed* are used for the noun in line 7.

Two adjectives describe the noun in line 7.

Mountain and Valley
by Glen Fry

Mountain

monstrous, humongous

towerring, jaged, wooded

high, U-shapped, glen, lowland

plowed, lying, farming

quiet low

Valley

The nouns in lines 1 and 7 are opposite.

As you write your first draft, ask yourself

★ **Subject:** What two nouns or topics am I focusing on?

★ **Audience:** Who will read my diamante?

★ **Purpose:** What is my goal in writing a diamante?

★ **Form:** What are the characteristics of a diamante?

Now, you're ready to write your own first draft. Review the words you listed on your rules organizer. Write down any new words that come to mind. Don't worry about the poem's diamond shape at this point. Use the Drafting Checklist as a guide.

Drafting Checklist

- Opposite nouns are written on lines 1 and 7.
- Adjectives are used on lines 2 and 6 to describe the nouns in lines 1 and 7.
- Lines 3 and 5 have words that end in <u>ing</u> or <u>ed</u> for each noun.
- Vivid words are used that quickly bring interesting images to mind.
- Figurative words may be used to bring the nouns to life.

Conferencing

Read your first draft to a partner. Does your partner like your choice of words? What words don't appeal to your partner? What words, if any, do you not like?

Writer's Tip
Write your draft, using every third line. This will give you extra room for revising and editing.

Tech Tip
Use one typeface for nouns, another for *ing* words, another for *ed* words, and so on. This will help you keep count for your poem.

Portfolio
Collect interesting words about your topic nouns. They'll be a good place to start when you revise your poem.

Take Another Look

Glen looked over his diamante. He liked some of his words. As he revised, he discarded a few words and thought of others. He reviewed the rules for writing a diamante and worked to make his images fit the rules. How did Glen's changes affect his diamante?

Take out words and choose new ones that also match the rules.

Add a vivid word and remove one.

Change words and move one word down a line.

Replace words with better ones.

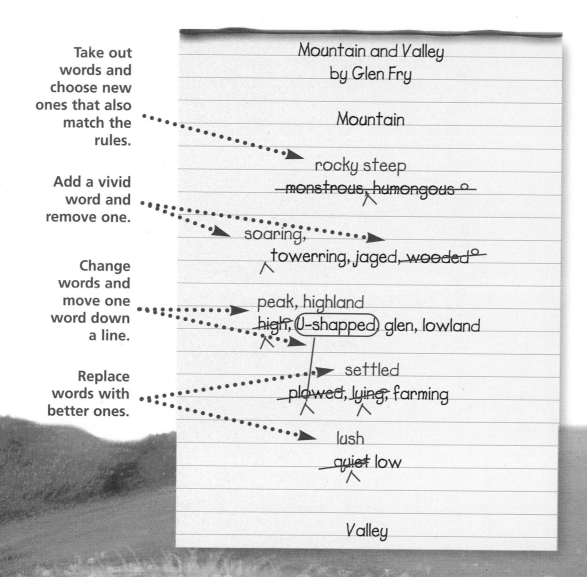

Mountain and Valley
by Glen Fry

Mountain

rocky steep
~~monstrous, humongous~~ ○

soaring,
towerring, jaged, ~~wooded~~ ○

peak, highland
~~high,~~ (U-shapped) glen, lowland

settled
~~plowed,~~ ~~lying,~~ farming

lush
~~quiet~~ low

Valley

Now start revising your poem. Read each line and check it against the rules for a diamante. The Revising Checklist will help you decide what changes to make. Mark your draft with these changes. Remember, you can revise your diamante more than once.

Revising Marks

≡	capitalize
∧	add
✐	remove
⊙	add a period
/	make lowercase
⌒	move
∼	transpose

Revising Checklist

- Does the poem begin and end with nouns that are really opposite in meaning?
- Does the diamante have the correct kinds of words, such as nouns or adjectives on the correct lines?
- Does the poem have the correct number of words on each line?
- Is the poem written in a lyric voice that helps to paint pictures with words?
- Does the poem use vivid words?
- Does the poem form a diamond shape?
- Do the words look and sound good together?

Tech Tip
The Format button or tool that centers words on the screen can help you put your poem in a diamond shape.

Conferencing

Read your diamante to a partner. Answer the Revising Checklist questions together. Discuss changes you could make for any part that gets a "no" answer. Take notes about these suggestions.

Portfolio
While you are waiting to edit, write down words that describe your nouns. Clip them to your revisions.

Become a Super Writer

To improve your diamante, keep thinking and writing in your lyric voice. For help, see the *Writer's Handbook* section, page 239.

Polish Your Writing

Glen made several revisions and was happy with his work. His diamante looked good. Then, he edited and proofread it. Notice the errors he found and corrected.

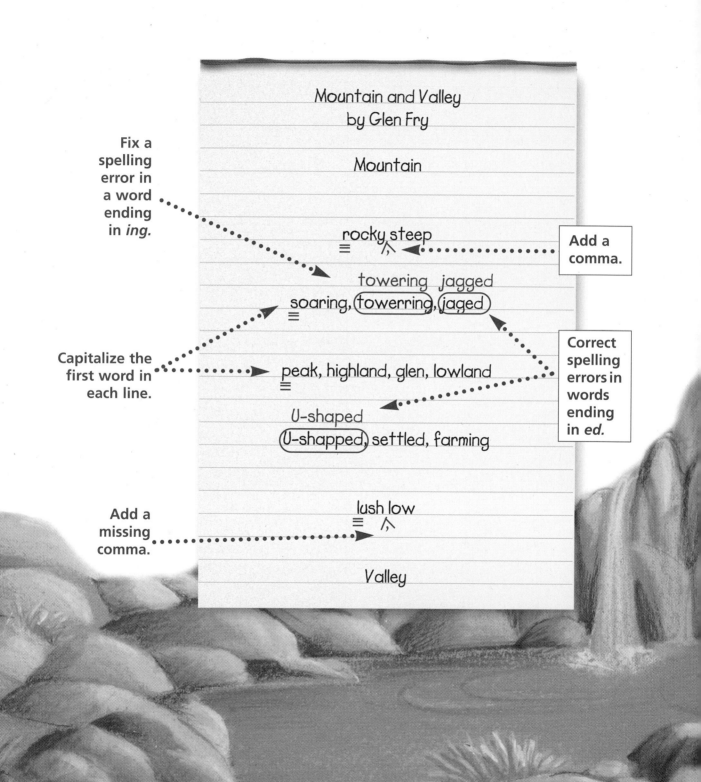

Mountain and Valley
by Glen Fry

Mountain

Fix a spelling error in a word ending in *ing.*

rocky steep

Add a comma.

towering   jagged
soaring, towerring, jaged

Capitalize the first word in each line.

peak, highland, glen, lowland

Correct spelling errors in words ending in *ed.*

U-shaped
U-shapped, settled, farming

Add a missing comma.

lush low

Valley

As you begin to edit and proofread your diamante, remember to make it as perfect as possible for it to be published. Use a different-colored pencil and the proofreading marks to show the changes you want to make. The Editing and Proofreading Checklist will help you.

Proofreading Marks

⁊	indent first line of paragraph
≡	capitalize
∧ or ∨	add
✗	remove
⊙	add a period
/	make lowercase
◯	spelling mistake
⌒	move
∾	transpose

Editing and Proofreading Checklist

- Are the words written so that they create a diamond-shaped poem?
- Is the first word in each line capitalized?
- Are there commas between each word in the poem?
- Are words with _ing_ and _ed_ endings spelled correctly?
  See the **Writer's Handbook** section, pages 276–277.
- Are all words spelled correctly?
  See the **Writer's Handbook** section, pages 275–284.
- Is the poem neat and easy to read?
  See the **Writer's Handbook** section, page 274.

Conferencing

Ask your partner to read your diamante. Can your partner find any grammar, punctuation, or spelling mistakes? Talk about any problems that are found and how to correct them.

Portfolio

Keep your lists and drafts until you are ready to publish. If you decide to change a word, check your lists.

Writer's Tip

If you're writing by hand, fold your paper in half the long way to make it easier to center the lines of the poem.

Become a Super Writer

Spelling words with the endings _ed_ and _ing_ can be tricky. Make your poem easy to read and understand by spelling these words correctly. See the _Writer's Handbook_ section, pages 276–277.

Share Your Work

Although Glen had written all of the early versions of his diamante by hand, he decided to use a computer to publish it. He began experimenting with different kinds of typefaces, or fonts. He used two fonts for the two parts of his poem. Decide for yourself if that was a good choice.

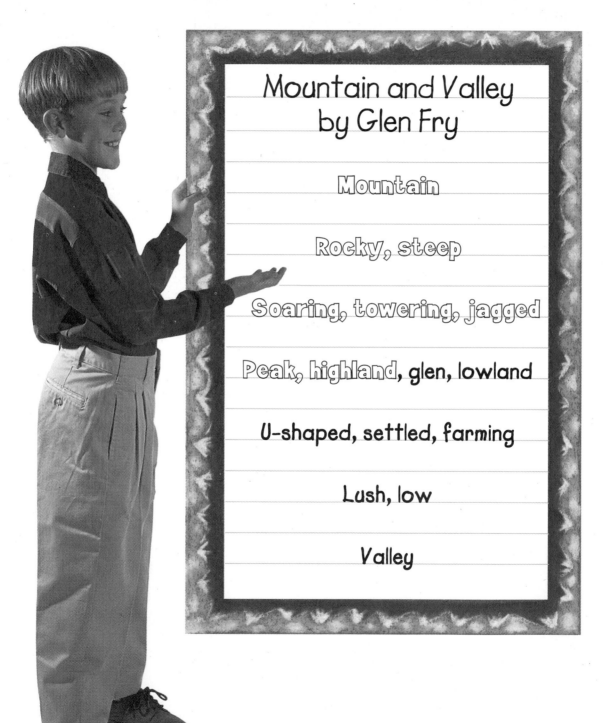

Mountain and Valley
by Glen Fry

Mountain

Rocky, steep

Soaring, towering, jagged

Peak, highland, glen, lowland

U-shaped, settled, farming

Lush, low

Valley

Glen decorated the page his poem was printed on and handed out copies to his classmates. Here are some other suggestions for sharing your diamante.

A Book of Diamonds ▶

Publish your diamante along with the poems your classmates wrote. You may wish to illustrate your poems. Glen Fry drew a border of mountains and valleys around his.

◀ Read Together

Form small groups for sharing your poetry. To help everyone concentrate on the poems, have one group member read his or her diamante aloud each day. If your poems were created on a computer, using different fonts, have a partner read the words in one typeface while you read the words in the second typeface.

Here's a Poem for You ▶

- Group the class's poems by similar subjects.
- Send each group's poems to an organization that might be interested in that subject. Perhaps the organization will publish them! For instance, if there's a national or state park in your area, try sending poems about nature to the park's manager.
- Be sure to include a letter that explains why you're sending the poems.

Sprouts!
Program
choolers!

s a new program
garden world
t sized growers.
gin in September
run throughout
beginning of
ember at the
Lincoln
Arboretum.

It is
designed
for children
s three through
dergarten. Young
for walks, create
many more fun
ession is one
hild must be
an adult. The
5.00 per child and

ore information
routs or for
tact the Park

Sprout
ule is:

Students of Jefferson Elementary Compose Diamantes in *Writers in the Park* Program

It is well known that writers often derive inspiration from their surroundings. Poets such as Walt Whitman and Emily Dickinson come to mind when one thinks of writers who were inspired by their natural surroundings. Susan Jones, a Language Arts teacher at Jefferson Elementary, felt that her students would benefit from the scenic environs of Lincoln Arboretum and so began the *Writers in the Park* Program. Once a month Ms. Jones' class visits the Arboretum grounds for some creative fuel for their writing exercises. This month their assignment was to write Diamantes, examples of which follow.

Plants
Green, leafy
Rooted, growing, dying
Everywhere, food, fewer, invisible
Playing, eating, scampering
Active, alive
Animals

Writing a Character Sketch

Will Rogers (1879–1935) was an American writer and performer who once said, "I never met a man I didn't like." A **character sketch** lets the writer describe someone he or she likes or thinks is special. In "Grandfather Foster," Lynn uses colorful words to tell about her grandfather.

Meet the Writer

I love everyone in my family, but I have a special place in my heart for Grandfather Foster. He is so special, I would like everyone to meet him.

Lynn Foster
Georgia

The writer tells what stands out most about the character.

Common and predicate adjectives help describe the person.

The character's actions are described.

Grandfather Foster
by Lynn Foster

Grandfather Foster is a man of few words but many thoughts. You know he thinks carefully about things just by the way he looks. His face is serious. Sometimes, his dark brown eyes twinkle when he laughs. He is not a tall person, but everyone notices when he is in the room.

Cooking is something that Grandfather Foster loves to do. He makes special meals like fried catfish. He grows his own fresh vegetables, including okra, beans, and corn. Someday, maybe he'll show me how to make peanut brittle.

My favorite times with Grandfather Foster, though, are when I get to visit him just by myself. We often sit on his front porch and read. Sometimes we take turns reading aloud to each other. Other times I tell him about what I am reading, and he tells me about what he's reading. He always listens to what I have to say.

My grandfather is kind and thoughtful and caring. That's why I'm happy that I'm a part of his life.

The end tells why the person is so special.

Talk About the Model

★ What words make you want to meet Lynn's grandfather?

★ How does Lynn grab your attention at the beginning of her character sketch?

★ What words does she use to describe her grandfather?

Make a Plan

Pick an Interesting Character

When it comes to a character sketch, deciding who you're going to write about is half the fun. Pick someone who interests you. If you prefer, think up an imaginary person.

Describe How Your Character Is Special

Make a character web to identify the important features of your character.

- Identify the most important thing you want the reader to know about your character.

- List physical details to show how the person acts, moves, and speaks.

- Include details about the person's personality and accomplishments.

- Use descriptive words that appeal to the senses.

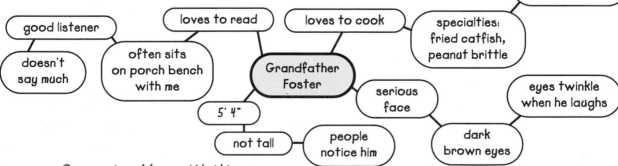

Organize Your Writing

Use a chart to organize your writing. Write notes to tell your character's name and most important feature in the beginning. Add notes to use sensory words as you describe your character in detail in the middle of your sketch. Note how you want to end your sketch— by telling why your character is so special.

Write It Down

First Impressions Count!

Grab your reader's attention.

- Introduce your character.
- Tell the most important thing you want the reader to know about him or her.

Keep Your Readers Interested

- Include details about the person. Describe what your character looks like and his or her favorite things, places, and activities.
- Use sensory words in your description.
- Present your details in an order that makes sense.

Bring Your Character Sketch to a Close

- Wrap up your description.
- End by giving a strong impression of the person or tell why the person is so special.

Tech Tip

Make a folder on a disk to store each piece of writing. Like a regular folder, it can hold all your typed notes and drafts.

Conferencing

Read your character sketch aloud to a partner. Does your partner get a solid impression of your subject? If not, what can you change or add?

Look It Over

Read your character sketch aloud to yourself.

- Check that you have the right adjectives and adverbs to describe your character.
- Look through a thesaurus to find better synonyms or antonyms for these words.
- Make sure you use the adjectives and adverbs correctly.
- This is the time to catch these and other mistakes in grammar and usage, spelling, and punctuation.
- Fix the things that don't sound quite right and that are incorrectly written.

Portfolio

If you like your character sketch, put it in a special section. Later on, revise, edit, proofread, and publish it.

Take a Closer Look

How are alligators and crocodiles alike and different? How do Earth and Mars compare? These are the kinds of questions that can be answered in compare-and-contrast essays. In a **compare-and-contrast essay,** you write about the things that are alike and different about two topics.

A Compare-and-Contrast Essay

★ **Clearly describes two topics by comparing how they are alike and different**

★ **Begins by identifying the two topics in the first paragraph**

★ **Groups facts and details about how the topics are alike and how they are different in separate paragraphs**

★ **Ends by summarizing the main points of how the topics are alike and different**

Meet the Writer

For comparing and contrasting, I couldn't think of anything to write about for the longest time. Then, I looked down at my desk, and there were my pencils!

Ramon Martinez
Texas

Prewriting

Think It Through

For a compare-and-contrast essay, start by identifying two topics that have something—but not everything—in common. For example, bike helmets may make you think of other kinds of helmets kids wear. A new video game may remind you of other video games you enjoy.

Brainstorming

One way to find a pair of topics is to brainstorm a pairs chart. Ramon listed items in his chart that are alike in some ways and different in others. Topic pairs can be objects, animals, people, or places.

> Think of as many pairs of items as you can that are alike and yet different. Write your pairs down. Use Ramon's chart as a guide.

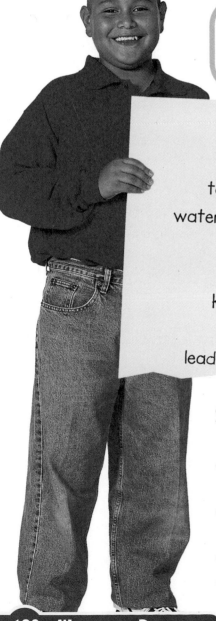

Ramon's Pairs Chart

desk	AND	chair
teacher	AND	scout leader
water skiing	AND	snow skiing
truck	AND	car
milk	AND	yogurt
kittens	AND	lion cubs
park	AND	school yard
lead pencil	AND	mechanical pencil

Select a Topic

Look at your chart.

- Try listing two ways in which each pair is alike and two ways in which each is different.
- If you notice only ways they are alike or only ways they are different, go on to another pair.
- Circle the pairs that give you enough to write about.
- Choose the one that interests you the most.

Design a Plan

Once you have a pair of topics in mind, you can begin to organize them. Venn diagrams are a good way to do that. In the middle, where the circles overlap, write how the two topics are similar. Outside that part, list how each topic is different.

Ramon chose to write about wooden and mechanical pencils. Here is the diagram that he made for his topics.

WOODEN PENCILS

Invented years ago

Made of wood

Need to sharpen

Have erasers

Use graphite

Bought in stores

Graphite breaks when you press hard on it

MECHANICAL PENCILS

Newer invention

Made of plastic

Click or twist to get lead

Create a Venn diagram for your topics.

- Observe the items. Take notes about what you see.
- Think about what your readers may want to know.
- For each feature you list for the first topic, list a similar or different feature for the second topic.
- Be as clear and specific as you can. Use precise and vivid words to tell all about your items.
- Order your information in a way that makes sense.

Conferencing

Share your Venn diagram with a partner or group. Are the topics you chose interesting to your partner? What other details does your partner think could be added?

Portfolio

Clip your Venn diagram to the other notes you made and store them in your portfolio.

Put It Into Words

When he started drafting, Ramon wrote quickly so he could get his thoughts down on paper. First, he wrote about similarities. Then, he started a new paragraph to write about differences. Finally, he wrote a conclusion. Here is his first draft.

Mechanical Pencils and Wooden Pencils
by Ramon Martinez

The topic is identified in the first paragraph.

Have you ever really thought about pencils? Most people haven't. They just use them. Pencils are important tools, though. People can buy a regular wooden pencil or a mechanical pencil. The wooden pencil often is called a "lead" pencil.

The second paragraph shows how the topics are alike.

Mechanical pencils and wooden pencils are alike. Both types of pencils have erasers at one end. Just in case someone makes a mistake. Both pencils have graphite. Both are something you can by in a store. The graphite in both pencils will break if you push down too hard on it.

The third paragraph has facts and details that show how the topics are different.

There are also differences between mechanical pencils and wooden pencils. Wooden pencils were invented many years ago, and mechanical pencils are newest. Regular pencils are carved wood that has graphite in the middle. Mechanical pencils are like pens. They're

The writer uses an example to help describe the pencils.

smooth and have a pocket clip on the side. You just have to tap, twist or click one to get the graphite to come out of mechanical pencils. Wooden pencils have to be sharpen.

The ideas are summarized, and the writer's viewpoint is given.

When I write, I prefer to use a brand-new wooden pencil. Sometimes I don't have a new pencil handy. Then, I use whatever kind of pencil I can find!

Think Like a Writer

As you write your first draft, ask yourself

★ **Subject:** What topics am I focusing on?

★ **Audience:** Will my audience understand what I am saying?

★ **Purpose:** What is my goal? Why am I writing?

★ **Form:** What are the characteristics of a compare-and-contrast essay?

Writer's Tip
Keep track of your progress. Put a check mark next to items on your Venn diagram when you finish writing about them.

Now you're ready to write the first draft of your compare-and-contrast essay. Review your Venn diagram and start writing. Remember, your purpose is to point out the similarities and differences between your two topics. Use the Drafting Checklist to help you.

Drafting Checklist

- The first paragraph identifies the two topics.
- Details about the topics' similarities are in one paragraph, and details about their differences are in another.
- The paragraphs begin with a sentence that states the main idea. Detail sentences follow.
- Descriptive details are added to make your meaning clear.
- Similes or metaphors can be used to compare or contrast your topics.
- The end summarizes your ideas and gives your point of view.

Tech Tip
Can you change the color of words on the screen? If so, make similarities one color and differences another.

Conferencing

Read your first draft to your partner. What does your partner think you can do to make your writing more interesting or more informative?

Portfolio

Clip your Venn diagram and your first draft together. If you can, store the items you're writing about, too.

Take Another Look

Ramon thought he had a good start on his essay. He liked what he had written but thought that it could be clearer. What did Ramon change in his essay? Do you think his changes made his piece clearer?

Use a variety of sentence types.

Make the beginning more precise.

Add information to clarify writing.

Use a transition to link ideas.

Make an idea clearer.

Replace and delete words to make the meaning clearer.

Mechanical Pencils and Wooden Pencils
by Ramon Martinez

Have you ever really thought about pencils? Most people haven't. They help us write messages, notes, letters, drafts, and many other things. They just use them. Pencils are important tools, though. People can

buy a regular wooden pencil or a mechanical pencil. The wooden

pencil often is called a "lead" pencil.

Mechanical pencils and wooden pencils are alike. Both types of

pencils have erasers at one end. Just in case someone makes a mistake.

in the center

Both pencils have graphite. Both are something you can by in a store.

Last of all,   when you write

The graphite in both pencils will break if you push down too hard on it.

There are also differences between mechanical pencils and

wooden pencils. Wooden pencils were invented many years ago, and

mechanical pencils are newest. Regular pencils are carved wood that

has graphite in the middle. Mechanical pencils are like pens. They're

smooth and have a pocket clip on the side. You just have to tap, twist

a mechanical pencil

or click one to get the graphite to come out of mechanical pencils.

Wooden pencils have to be sharpen.

When I write, I prefer to use a brand-new wooden pencil.

Sometimes I don't have a new pencil handy. Then, I use whatever kind

of pencil I can find!

See what revisions you would like to make. Read your first draft slowly. As you find something you want to change, mark the corrections on the page.

Keep rereading your essay as you make changes to be sure it still makes sense. Don't stop until you really like what you've done with it. Use the Revising Checklist to help you make changes.

Revising Marks

≡	capitalize
∧	add
ϼ	remove
⊙	add a period
/	make lowercase
◯	move
∼	transpose

Revising Checklist

- Does the essay have a beginning, a middle, and an end?
- Are the similarities and differences presented in separate paragraphs?
- Are there enough facts and details to make the comparisons interesting?
- Are transitions used to link ideas?
- Are a variety of interrogative, exclamatory, imperative, and declarative sentences used?

Tech Tip
Use the Cut and Paste tools when you have to cut a lot of words. To remove just a few letters, it's faster to use the Delete key.

Conferencing

Read your compare-and-contrast essay to a partner. Then, go over the Revising Checklist together. Take notes as you talk about what you could change to make your essay clearer.

Portfolio
Save your revisions in your portfolio until you are ready to edit and proofread your writing.

Become a Super Writer

Transitions can give your paragraphs a sense of unity. For help in using transitions, see the *Writer's Handbook* section, page 237.

Polish Your Writing

Ramon was almost finished. Just one more look to correct a few small things, and his essay would be perfect. What changes did Ramon make to this part of his essay? How did his changes help his essay?

Mechanical Pencils and Wooden Pencils
by Ramon Martinez

Have you ever really thought about pencils? Most people haven't. They just use them. Pencils are important tools, though. They help us write messages, notes, letters, drafts, and many other things. People can buy a regular wooden pencil or a mechanical pencil. The wooden pencil often is called a "lead" pencil.

Mechanical pencils and wooden pencils are alike in several ways. **Correct a sentence fragment.** Both types of pencils have erasers at one end. Just in case someone makes a mistake. Both pencils have graphite in the center. Both are **Correct a misspelled homonym.** something you can ~~by~~ buy in a store. Last of all, the graphite in both pencils will break if you push down too hard on it when you write.

There are also differences between mechanical pencils and wooden pencils. Wooden pencils were invented many years ago, and **Fix a comparative adjective that's used incorrectly.** newer mechanical pencils are ~~newest~~. Regular pencils are carved wood that has graphite in the middle. Mechanical pencils are like pens. They're smooth and have a pocket clip on the side. You just have to **Insert a comma in the series of actions.** tap, twist, or click a mechanical pencil to get the graphite to come **Add the correct past-tense ending to the verb.** out. Wooden pencils have to be ~~sharpen~~ sharpened.

Now it's your turn to edit and proofread your writing. Take your time. If you rush, you might miss mistakes you would usually catch. Use the proofreading marks so you will know at a glance what corrections to make. This Editing and Proofreading Checklist will help you.

Proofreading Marks

Mark	Meaning
⁋	indent first line of paragraph
≡	capitalize
∧ or ∨	add
⌿	remove
⊙	add a period
/	make lowercase
◯	spelling mistake
⌒	move
∾	transpose

Editing and Proofreading Checklist

- Did I spell all words correctly?
  See pages 275–284 in the *Writer's Handbook* section.
- Did I make comparisons with adjectives and adverbs correctly?
  See pages 258 and 260 in the *Writer's Handbook* section.
- Did I use commas and other punctuation correctly?
  See pages 269–273 in the *Writer's Handbook* section.
- Is my copy neat and easy to read?
  See "Handwriting and Format" on page 274 in the *Writer's Handbook* section.

Conferencing

Have your partner read your essay. Go over the checklist questions together and mark extra changes you wish to make. Ask if your partner found other kinds of mistakes.

Writer's Tip
Keep a dictionary handy to check the spelling of words you're not sure of.

Portfolio
Don't forget to clip all your drafts together. Put your final copy on the top of the pile. Mark it with today's date.

Become a Super Writer

Adjectives and adverbs can be used to make comparisons. They add interest to your writing. For help, see pages 258 and 260 in the *Writer's Handbook* section.

Share Your Work

Ramon's finished compare-and-contrast essay shows that you don't have to use a complicated topic. A writer who is a good observer can compare and contrast even two very common objects. His revisions produced a nicely "sharpened" final piece!

Mechanical Pencils and Wooden Pencils
by Ramon Martinez

Have you ever really thought about pencils? Most people haven't. They just use them. Pencils are important tools, though. They help us write messages, notes, letters, drafts, and many other things. People can buy a regular wooden pencil or a mechanical pencil. The wooden pencil often is called a "lead" pencil.

Mechanical pencils and wooden pencils are alike in several ways. Both types of pencils have erasers at one end in case someone makes a mistake. Both pencils have graphite in the center. Both are something you can buy in a store. Last of all, the graphite in both pencils will break if you push down too hard on it when you write.

There are also differences between mechanical pencils and wooden pencils. Wooden pencils were invented many years ago, and mechanical pencils are newer. Regular pencils are carved wood that has graphite in the middle. Mechanical pencils are like pens. They're smooth and have a pocket clip on the side. You just have to tap, twist, or click a mechanical pencil to get the graphite to come out. Wooden pencils have to be sharpened.

When I write, I prefer to use a brand-new wooden pencil. Sometimes I don't have a new pencil handy. Then, I use whatever kind of pencil I can find!

Now, it's your turn to share your compare-and-contrast essay with your classmates. Here are some suggestions for publishing it.

Seeing Is Believing ▶

Create a tri-fold display featuring your published essay and the items you wrote about. Ramon brought in examples of both kinds of pencils to display with his published piece. However, if you wrote about lions and tigers, pictures would be preferable to the actual items.

◀ Make a Book

Work with your classmates to publish a book of compare-and-contrast essays.

- Divide up the work among different committees.
- Include interesting photos and illustrations.
- Think of a title and a design for the cover and how the book could be printed.

Be an Expert Witness ▶

Pretend that you have been requested to formally present your views on your subject to a group of very important people— your classmates.

- Read your essay aloud or make notes and speak from them.
- Consider videotaping your presentation. You can view it later to see for yourself if your presentation was convincing.

Writing an Eyewitness Account

Can you imagine what it's like to watch history being made? An **eyewitness account** is written by someone who actually saw an event happen. In it, the writer shares what he or she saw, heard, and felt as the event took place.

In 1968, Anne Morrow Lindbergh watched *Apollo 8* set out on its mission to orbit the moon. The following account of that launch is from her book *Earth Shine*.

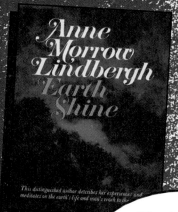

Talk About the Model

As a Reader

★ How does the writer convince you that she was an eyewitness to the launch?

★ What do you think the writer felt about the launch? What in her writing tells you her feelings?

As a Writer

★ How did the writer order the events in her account?

★ How did the writer describe the launch so that you felt as if you were present at it?

from *Earth Shine*
by Anne Morrow Lindbergh

People stop talking, stand in front of their cars, and raise binoculars to their eyes. We peer nervously at the launch site and then at our wrist watches. Radio voices blare unnaturally loud from car windows. "Now only thirty minutes to launch . . . fifteen minutes . . . six minutes . . . thirty seconds to go . . . twenty . . . T minus fifteen . . . fourteen . . . thirteen . . . twelve . . . eleven . . . ten . . . nine . . . Ignition!"

A jet of steam shoots from the pad below the rocket. "Ahhhh!" The crowd gasps, almost in unison. Now great flames spurt, leap, belch out across the horizon. Clouds of smoke billow up on either side of the rocket, completely hiding its base. From the midst of this holocaust, the rocket begins to rise—slowly, as in a dream, so slowly it seems to hang suspended on the cloud of fire and smoke. It's impossible—it can't rise. Yes, it rises, but heavily, as if the giant weight is pulled by an invisible hand out of the atmosphere, like the lead on a plumb line from the depths of the sea. Slowly it rises and—because of our distance—silently as in a dream.

The writer uses details to describe events just before the launch.

The writer tells what she saw and heard during liftoff.

The sequence of events is told in order.

The writer uses a metaphor to make a comparison.

The writer's feelings and personal reactions are described.

The writer uses a simile to make a comparison.

Make a Plan

Choose an Event

Decide on an event for your eyewitness account. It should be something you've actually watched happening—a dramatic event like a fire or a bike race or a more ordinary event that you think will be interesting to others.

Quick Write the Details

Jot down what you saw. Write as many facts, details, thoughts, and feelings as you can.

Organize Your Writing

Next, write a simple outline. Organize your information into main topics based on the order of events. Tell what happened first, next, and last. Later, these main topics will become your paragraphs.

BORMAN LOVELL ANDERS

Write It Down

Ready, set, write!

- Follow your outline.
- Write down everything you saw, heard, and felt at the event in the order that things happened.
- Include as many details as possible. Use similes and metaphors if possible.
- End your account by telling how you felt.

Tech Tip

As you revise, use different colors or typefaces for new words to see which words improve your writing.

Conferencing

Read your account to a partner or group. Is any information out of order. Are more details needed?

Portfolio

Keep your outline and drafts. You may decide that you would like to publish your eyewitness account.

Look It Over

Reread your writing. Can you use time-order words, such as *first* and *next,* to help organize your details? Are there problem words, such as *there*, *their*, and *they're,* that should be checked for spelling? Go back and change anything that is not just right.

JUST THE FACTS

Writing to Inform

133

Writing an Informative Paragraph

Meet the Writer

I heard about this strange plant. So I did some research and learned all about it. This is what I wrote to share what I discovered.

Lee Pak
Oregon

Do you like to read about how things work or explain something you know well? One of the best tools for learning or teaching things is an informative paragraph. An **informative paragraph** gives facts and details about a topic.

Lee gives lots of interesting information about the Venus's-flytrap in his paragraph. His facts and details inform the reader about this most unusual plant.

Fantastic Meat-Eating Plant
by Lee Pak

One of the strangest plants you'll ever hear about grows in North Carolina and South Carolina. The plant's name is Venus's-flytrap, and here's what's amazing about it—it eats insects and small animals. The outside of each of its leaves is shaped to form a trap. Inside the leaf, there are trigger hairs. The plant has a sweet liquid that creatures love. When insects or small animals come to get it, they usually land on one of the plant's leaves. This sets off the trigger hairs, so the leaf closes around the helpless creature. Sharp spines on the edges of the leaf keep the creature from escaping. After the Venus's flytrap eats its victim, the leaf reopens and is ready to trap another creature.

Talk About the Model

★ What is the main idea of the paragraph?

★ What facts and details does the writer add to help explain the topic?

Tech Tip
Use the Tab key each time you want to indent a new paragraph.

Make a Plan

Plan your own informative paragraph.

- Make a list of topics that interest you. Look through your Learning Log or Observation Log for ideas.

- Choose a topic that you can tell about in one paragraph.

- Find information about your topic, and jot down details that support your main idea.

- Use a cluster diagram, an idea list, or an inverted triangle to organize your information.

Venus's-flytrap eats insects and small animals

Leaf's shape forms a trap

Plant makes a liquid insects like

Trigger hairs and spines trap insect

Write It Down

Now start writing.

- Begin with a topic sentence that summarizes your main idea.

- Give facts and details to support your main idea and help your reader understand.

- Use time-order words like *first, next,* and *finally* if they make it easier for your reader to follow along.

Write clearly and, if possible, use examples to explain.

Conferencing

Read your informative paragraph to a partner. Ask if your paragraph is clear and easy to follow. Can your partner identify the main idea?

Look It Over

Set your work aside for a while. Then, reread it carefully. Do you explain things enough? Is your paragraph clear and easy to understand? Do your sentences' subjects and verbs agree? Mark changes on your draft in case you decide to publish.

Portfolio

Store your notes and drafts in your portfolio. Later on, you might want to use them in a longer report.

Writing Directions and Instructions

Meet the Writer

Julie Agnone lives in Virginia. She works as an editor and a writer and enjoys hiking and swimming.

Have you ever gotten lost trying to follow **directions**? Sometimes a whole step is missing or it's too difficult to follow. That's why good writers try to keep step-by-step **instructions** as simple and clear as possible.

Julie Agnone's directions for layering liquids were published in *National Geographic World* and show you about an important idea in science.

NATIONAL GEOGRAPHIC
world

Heating Up Summer
WILDFIRE!
When
ALBERT EINSTEIN
Was a Kid

VACATION SENSATIONS
• River Rapids
• Highway Giants

ENDANGERED: Wild Dogs

One of the things I like about writing for kids is that I'm able to make learning fun.

Layered Liquids
by Julie Agnone

Have you heard the saying "oil and water don't mix"? In fact, oil, water, corn syrup, and glycerin don't mix. To check this statement, do this experiment. Gather the ingredients needed, then follow the steps carefully.

> **The writer tells what is needed.**

Ingredients

- ❑ light corn syrup
- ❑ glycerin
- ❑ water
- ❑ vegetable oil
- ❑ measuring cup
- ❑ 4 clean containers

- ❑ blue and red food coloring
- ❑ tall, clear glass or jar
- ❑ funnel
- ❑ sink for washing funnel

> **The writer tells where to get uncommon items.**

1. Measure 1/3 cup (.08 L) each of light corn syrup, glycerin (available at drugstores), water, and vegetable oil into separate containers.

> **Step-by-step directions are given.**

2. Use food coloring to color the corn syrup red and the water blue. Do not color the oil or glycerin.

3. Pour the red syrup into a tall, clear glass or jar. Try not to let it dribble down the sides.

> **The directions are clear and precise.**

4. Use a funnel to pour the glycerin down the inside of the glass. Pour carefully to avoid disturbing the bottom layer. Wash the funnel.

> **Time-order words make the directions easy to understand.**

5. Repeat step 4, first adding the blue water, then the oil, washing the funnel between steps. The liquids will stay in separate layers if you are careful not to shake the glass.

Why? Each liquid has its own density, or weight. You added liquids in order from highest to lowest density. The oil stays on top because it is least dense.

> **The conclusion explains why something happens.**

Talk About the Model

As a Reader

★ Do you think the instructions are clear?

★ Would you find it easy to do this experiment? Why or why not?

As a Writer

★ Did the writer list the steps in order? How do you know?

★ Why did the writer use imperative sentences throughout?

★ Why does the writer explain what happens in the end?

Make a Plan

Before you write directions or instructions, you need to choose a topic and then brainstorm a list of steps to follow.

Identify Something You Know Really Well

Think of things that you know how to do or make. You could even choose something you know how to cook!

● Brainstorm a list of things you can do or make.

● Consider whether or not you could tell someone how to make or do these things.

● If you find that you don't know or can't remember how to do a certain step, cross that topic off your list.

● Choose a topic that interests you from those that are left.

Step by Step

Think about your topic and how to explain it.

● Picture each step in your mind.

● Then, list all the steps.

● Use as many steps as you need.

● Review your list. If any steps are missing, add them.

● Make a list of all the ingredients or materials needed.

● Lastly, think about how you could introduce your instructions and how you could conclude them.

Design a Plan

Organize your steps by using a flowchart.

- Start with a title.
- Add your introduction and ingredients.
- Then, list each step in order.
- Add a conclusion that explains what should happen and why.
- Check the order of your plan. Does it make sense?

Title → Introduction → Ingredients → Steps → Conclusion

Write It Down

Once you have finished your plan, you can begin to write your directions or instructions.

- Follow your plan.
- Use "Layered Liquids" as a model.
- Keep your writing simple, clear, and precise.
- Use imperative sentences for each step.
- Don't add too many details.
- Number your steps and use time-order words to help your readers follow the steps.
- Add a statement at the end that tells your readers what to expect if they follow your directions, or why you wrote the directions the way you did.

Tech Tip
Use boldface type to call attention to words or phrases that you think are important.

Conferencing

Ask a partner to read over your writing. Could your partner follow your directions or instructions? Do you need to add or take out any information?

Look It Over

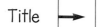

Store your list, flowchart, and directions. Your class might want to publish a book of things to do and make.

Double-check your directions or instructions to make sure they are simple and easy to follow. Have you included only necessary information? Are the steps in the correct order? If you plan to publish your work, remember to revise, edit, and proofread your writing.

A Nose for News

Writers who sniff out good news stories are often called news hounds. As soon as something happens, they find out what happened, who was involved, and when, where, and why it happened. Then, they rush back and write a **news story.**

A News Story

★ Uses information from interviews, reading, and observations

★ Gives facts, not opinions, about something that happened

★ Clearly focuses on the *who, what, where, when,* and *why* of the story

★ Has a headline that captures the reader's attention

★ Includes a byline that tells who wrote the story

★ Begins with a lead paragraph that sums up the most important information in the story

★ Adds information and details in the body of the story, in order from most important to least important

Meet the Writer

I enjoy the news because I like to know what is going on. I wrote this news story about something that happened in Georgia, where my cousins live.

Megan Wingard
Pennsylvania

Think It Through

A news story reports facts about an event that just took place. When you write a news story, first, choose a topic. Then, gather the information you need to write about it.

Brainstorming

News is all around you. Just keep your eyes open and think. Check your Observation Log and journal, too.

Brainstorm news items about your school, community, favorite sports, or other topics. Take notes on the topics that interest you.

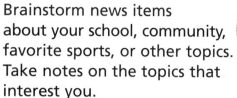

Megan's Notes
- soccer—U.S. national team prepares for big games
- weather—tornado turns out to be an F-5

Select a Topic

Study your notes and ask yourself the questions below. Then, pick the news item you think would make the best story.

- Which item would you and your readers want to find out more about?
- What facts do you already know about this news event?
- Where can you get the rest of the information you need?

Gather Information

The places where you get information and the people you interview are called news sources. Use sources you can trust.

- Ask questions. Interview those involved— eyewitnesses, police officers, and experts.
- Use note cards to record their exact words.
- Make observations and take careful notes.
- Read for background information. Take notes.

Design a Plan

Once you have gathered information and taken notes for your news story, make your plan. Megan decided to write about a tornado that struck Georgia. She found some good facts and a quotation for her news story. Then, she organized her notes into this plan. It shows her story's headline, lead paragraph, and body.

The headline gives the main facts and gets the reader's attention. ••••▶ Headline: Tornado in Georgia

The lead paragraph gives the 5 *W*'s— *who, what, when, where,* **and** *why.* ••••▶ Lead paragraph: Severe thunderstorms cause a tornado that hits Georgia on April 9; 15 people dead; houses wrecked

The body gives more information in order from most important to least important. ••••▶ Body: Quotation from survivor; report of tornado siren going off 19 times; F-4, then F-5 on scale; explanation of Fujita scale; people left to clean up or start over

When you have the facts you need, make your plan. Use Megan's model and these questions to help you.

- What happened? What are the main facts in your news story?
- Who was involved, and where and when did the news item take place?
- Why did the news item take place?
- What other information is important for your readers to know?

Conferencing

Ask a partner to look at your plan. Does your lead paragraph contain the 5 *W*'s? Are the facts in the body organized from most important to least important?

Portfolio

Store your notes and plan. Refer to them when you write your first draft.

NEWS STORY Drafting

Put It Into Words

Megan was eager to get her story down on paper. She reviewed her plan and then wrote quickly. Here is her first draft.

The headline grabs the reader's attention.

Tornado in Georgia

The lead paragraph tells *who, why, what, when,* and *where.*

Severe thunderstorms caused a tornado to go through parts of northern Georgia on April 9, 1998. Fifteen people lost their lives. Homes were ripped apart, trees were snapped in two, bad floods occurred.

The body of the story presents more information and details.

Some people says that they heard the tornado siren go off 19 times. At first, they thought it was an F-4 on the Fujita scale. Then they found out it was an F-5. The Fujita scale measures how damaging a tornado is. An F-4 tornado can throw and destroy a car. It has winds from 207 to 260 miles per hour. An F-5 can make a car seem like a missile. It's winds are 261 to 318 miles per hour.

A transition word links ideas.

The writer reports what an eyewitness said.

One woman said, we were awakened by a loud rumble. My husband and I ran to the basement. Then the tornado tore off our roof!

The writer describes events in the order in which they happened.

The Red Cross opened sevarel shelters to help people. They served close to 3,000 emergency meals two days after the tornado.

The writer tells the tornado's effects on people's lives.

All that the residents of Georgia now can do is start cleaning up. Some will have to begin a new life in a new home. Some have lost nieghbors, friends, and loved ones.

Think Like a Writer

As you write your first draft, ask yourself

★ **Subject:** What event am I focusing on?

★ **Audience:** Who will be reading my news story?

★ **Purpose:** Why am I writing this news story? What is my goal?

★ **Form:** What are the characteristics of a news story?

Writer's Tip
To make sure you include everything you need, label the parts of your news story in the margin. Also label the 5 *W*'s.

Review your information, and then begin writing the first draft of your news story. Follow the plan you made and use your notes. Concentrate on getting the facts and details written down in an order that makes sense. Use the following Drafting Checklist as a guide.

Tech Tip
Center your headline and put it in large type. Pick a typeface that matches the spirit of your news story.

Drafting Checklist

- The news story has an eye-catching headline.
- The lead paragraph answers the 5 <u>W</u>'s—<u>who</u>, <u>what</u>, <u>when</u>, <u>where</u>, and <u>why</u>.
- The body presents information and details in order from most important to least important.
- Only reliable facts, quotations, and information from interviews, observations, and background reading are used.

Conferencing

Read your draft to a partner. Does your partner think you followed the correct format for a news story? Are there facts that need to be added, deleted, or reordered?

Portfolio

Label any computer disks you've used and keep them in your portfolio.

Take Another Look

Megan liked her news story when she reread it, but she saw some sections she wanted to rework. Look at Megan's draft below. What revisions did she make? How do you think they improved her news story?

Revise headline to use better words.

rips through

Tornado in Georgia

Add byline to tell who wrote the news story.

by Megan Wingard

Severe thunderstorms caused a tornado to go through parts

blast

Replace an overused verb with a vivid verb for variety.

of northern Georgia on April 9, 1998. Fifteen people lost their

lives. Homes were ripped apart, trees were snapped in two, bad

floods occurred.

Some people says that they heard the tornado siren go off

19 times. At first, they thought it was an F-4 on the Fujita

scale. Then they found out it was an F-5. The Fujita scale measures

how damaging a tornado is. An F-4 tornado can throw and destroy

Move sentences to improve order.

a car. It has winds from 207 to 260 miles per hour. An F-5 can make

a car seem like a missile. It's winds are 261 to 318 miles per hour.

One woman said, we were awakened by a loud rumble. My husband

and I ran to the basement. Then the tornado tore off our roof!

Add adverb to tell how something happens.

quickly

The Red Cross opened sevarel shelters to help people. They

served close to 3,000 emergency meals two days after the tornado.

Change word order in sentence to improve sequence.

All that the residents of Georgia now can do is start cleaning up.

Some will have to begin a new life in a new home. Some have lost

nieghbors, friends, and loved ones.

Read your draft to see what changes you want to make to improve your writing. Remember, you can use your margins for notes and to try out new words and sentences. If you need more information, check your prewriting notes. Use the Revising Checklist to help you make changes.

Revising Marks

≡	capitalize
∧	add
⌒	remove
⊙	add a period
/	make lowercase
◠	move
∾	transpose

Revising Checklist

- Does the news story have a headline and a beginning that grab the reader's attention?
- Are there enough facts and details to involve the reader in the story?
- Are facts used and not opinions?
- Are events presented in the order in which they happened?
- Are precise and vivid words used to make the story interesting to read?
- Have I used adverbs correctly to tell <u>where</u>, <u>when</u>, and <u>how</u>?
- Have I included a byline?

Conferencing

With a partner, read and discuss your news story. If either of you thinks that the answer to any question in the Revising Checklist is "no," talk about how you can revise your writing to improve it. Take notes as you respond to your partner's suggestions.

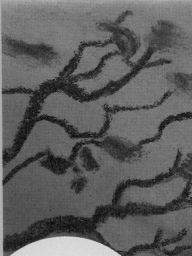

Tech Tip
Adjust your margins or set your story in columns so that it looks like an article in your favorite newspaper.

Portfolio
Save your drafts and notes. You can review them just before you edit and proofread your news story.

★ Become a Super Writer

To give your news story more detail and reader interest, use adverbs that tell *where*, *when*, and *how*. For help with adverbs, see the *Writer's Handbook* section, page 259.

Polish Your Writing

It's easy to make mistakes when you are concentrating on what you want to say. That's why writers edit and proofread their work. Notice what Megan corrected when she polished her news story and the proofreading marks she used.

Capitalize the headline.

Tornado rips through Georgia
by Megan Wingard

Severe thunderstorms caused a tornado to blast through parts

Add a conjunction.

of northern Georgia on April 9, 1998. Fifteen people lost their

Capitalize the first word in a direct quotation and place quotation marks around eyewitness's exact words.

lives. Homes were ripped apart, trees were snapped in two, bad
                                                              and

floods occurred.

One woman said, we were awakened by a loud rumble. My

husband and I ran to the basement. Then the tornado tore off our
                              said
roof! Some people says that they heard the tornado siren go off 19

Correct a verb form.

times. At first, they thought it was an F-4 on the Fujita scale. Then

they found out it was an F-5. The Fujita scale measures how

damaging a tornado is. An F-4 tornado can throw and destroy a

Replace the contraction with the possessive pronoun Its.

car. It has winds from 207 to 260 miles per hour. An F-5 can make a
                              Its
car seem like a missile. It's winds are 261 to 318 miles per hour.

Correct a misspelled word.

                                        several
The Red Cross quickly opened sevarel shelters to help people.

They served close to 3,000 emergency meals two days after the

Add a comma after an introductory word.

tornado. Now all that the residents of Georgia can do is start

Correct a misspelled word.

cleaning up. Some will have to begin a new life in a new home. Some
           neighbors
have lost nieghbors, friends, and loved ones.

Go ahead and polish your news story now. Review it for grammar, usage, mechanics, and spelling. Look up problem words in a dictionary. Then, use proofreading marks to show the changes you want to make. You can use the Editing and Proofreading Checklist as a guide.

Editing and Proofreading Checklist

- Did I capitalize my headline correctly?

  See the **Writer's Handbook** section, page 266.

- Did I use quotation marks to enclose a speaker's exact words?

  See the **Writer's Handbook** section, page 273.

- Did I use periods and apostrophes correctly?

  See the **Writer's Handbook** section, pages 269 and 272.

- Did I use adverbs that tell <u>where</u>, <u>when</u>, and <u>how</u> correctly?

  See the **Writer's Handbook** section, page 259.

- Did I spell all the words correctly?

  See the **Writer's Handbook** section, pages 275–284.

Conferencing

Have your partner read your news story and check for mistakes. Talk about any errors in grammar and usage, punctuation, capitalization, and spelling that are found. Take notes, and then mark additional corrections on your draft.

Tech Tip

Use the spelling- and grammar-checking features on your word processor to double-check your work.

Become a Super Writer

Some newspapers and magazines may capitalize their headlines differently. One way is to capitalize just the first, last, and main words in the headline. For help, see the *Writer's Handbook* section, page 266.

Portfolio

Make a file for your first draft, revisions, and notes. Review these items before you publish your news story.

NEWS STORY Publishing

Share Your Work

Megan had put a lot of work into her news story. Here is her final copy, which her teacher posted on the school's community-news bulletin board.

Tornado Rips Through Georgia
by Megan Wingard

Severe thunderstorms caused a tornado to blast through parts of northern Georgia on April 9, 1998. Fifteen people lost their lives. Homes were ripped apart, trees were snapped in two, and bad floods occurred.

One woman said, "We were awakened by a loud rumble. My husband and I ran to the basement. Then the tornado tore off our roof!" Some people said that they heard the tornado siren go off 19 times. At first, they thought it was an F-4 on the Fujita scale. Then they found out it was an F-5. The Fujita scale measures how damaging a tornado is. An F-4 tornado can throw and destroy a car. It has winds from 207 to 260 miles per hour. An F-5 can make a car seem like a missile. Its winds are 261 to 318 miles per hour.

The Red Cross quickly opened several shelters to help people. They served close to 3,000 emergency meals two days after the tornado. Now, all that the residents of Georgia can do is start cleaning up. Some will have to begin a new life in a new home. Some have lost neighbors, friends, and loved ones.

News stories are supposed to be shared and appreciated. Here are some suggestions for publishing the news story you wrote.

Read All About It ▶

Make a clean final copy of your news story. Then, post it with stories by several of your classmates. Change and add stories each day so that people in your school can keep up with interesting news from all over.

◀ On the Air

Pretend that you are an anchor person on a network news show. Copy your story onto index cards. Practice reading your news story aloud. Then, present your news story in a "News Center" show.

Class Paper ▶

Create a newspaper featuring all the news stories written by your classmates. Use real photos and original illustrations with captions you write. Try out different typefaces in different sizes for headlines to make it look like a real newspaper. Design a layout of the pages that makes every news story seem important.

Writing a Business or Formal Letter

Meet the Writer

My teacher told us that kids who write business letters are taken seriously. I hope so, because I really want to know more about the Oceanarium in Maine.

Matthew Langdon
Florida

Suppose you wanted to complain to someone about your new sneakers that fell apart after being worn for two days. Maybe you need information about a particular organization or company. Writing a **business letter** is one of the best ways to get the results you want.

Matthew wrote his letter to get more information about the Mount Desert Oceanarium, in Maine. He used formal language and a businesslike tone.

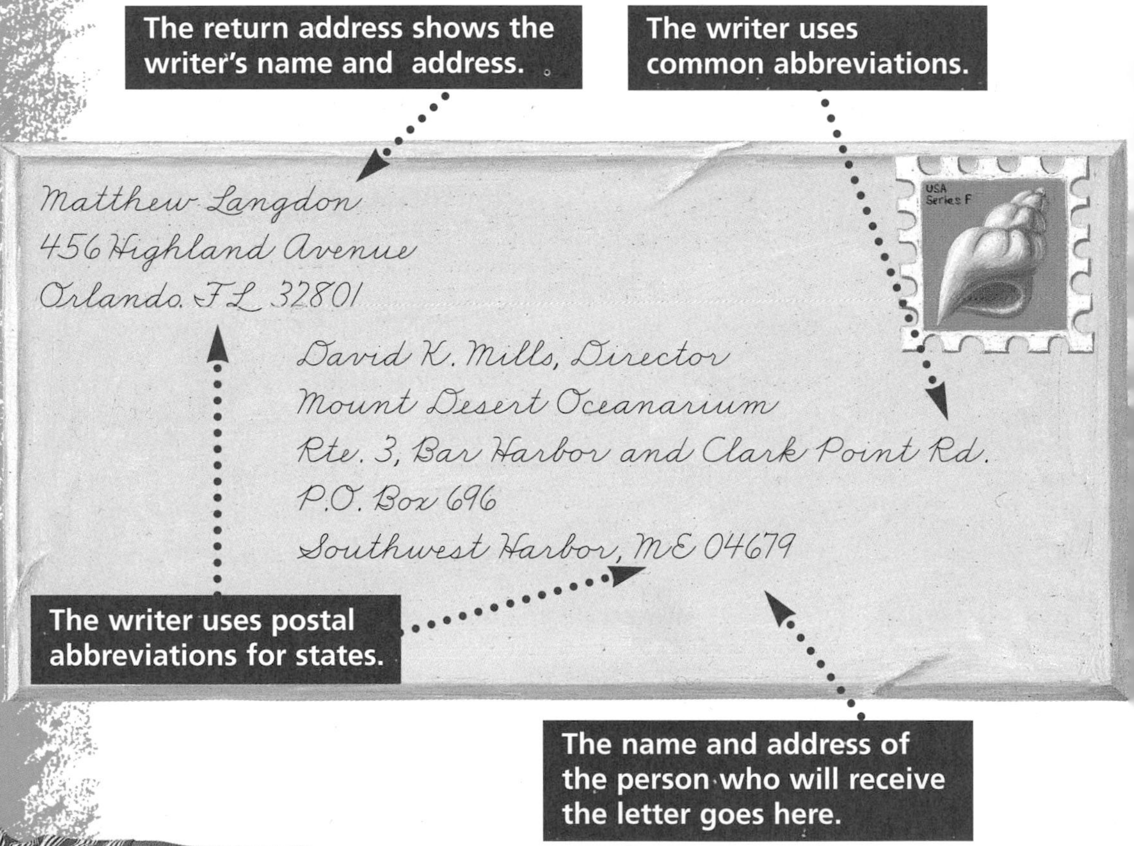

The return address shows the writer's name and address.
The writer uses common abbreviations.
Matthew Langdon
456 Highland Avenue
Orlando, FL 32801
USA
Series F
David K. Mills, Director
Mount Desert Oceanarium
Rte. 3, Bar Harbor and Clark Point Rd.
P.O. Box 696
Southwest Harbor, ME 04679
The writer uses postal abbreviations for states.
The name and address of the person who will receive the letter goes here.

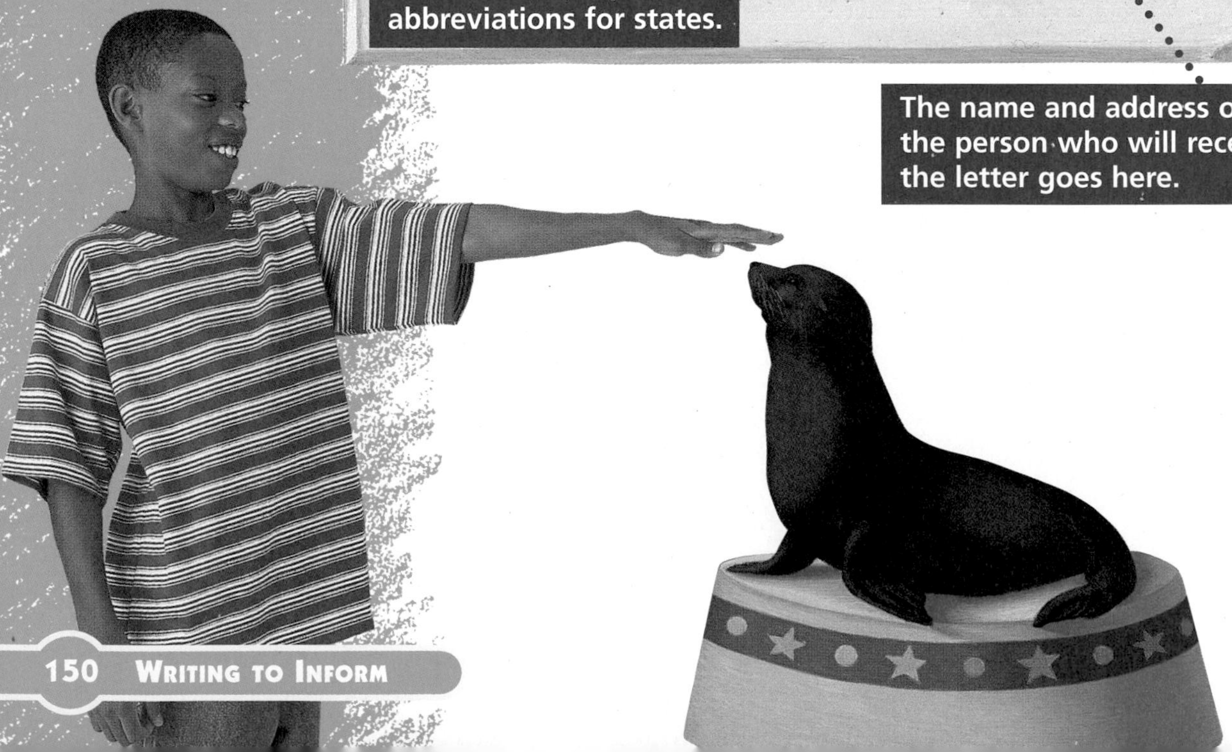

Talk About the Model

★ What reason does the writer give for writing the letter?

★ How does the writer get his reader's attention?

★ How would you describe the language in the letter?

456 Highland Avenue
Orlando, FL 32801
April 18, 1999

Heading: This gives the writer's return address and today's date.

David K. Mills, Director
Mount Desert Oceanarium
Rte. 3, Bar Harbor and Clark Point Rd.
P.O. Box 696
Southwest Harbor, ME 04679

Inside Address: This tells where the letter will go—the person and his or her title, the company name, and the mailing address.

Dear Mr. Mills:

Salutation: The writer puts the greeting *Dear* before the person's name and places a colon after it.

My family and I will be visiting Maine this summer. We will be camping on Mount Desert Island. I am excited about our trip because I am very interested in sea life.

I've seen sharks and dolphins at Marineland in St. Augustine, Florida, and at the Miami Seaquarium. It's exciting to see sea life up close in real ocean tanks.

That is why I am writing to you. I would like to know more about the Mount Desert Oceanarium. I learned from the Internet that you have ocean tanks for seals and lobsters. What other kinds of sea life do you have? Also, do you have guided tours?

Could you please send me a brochure and any other information you have about the oceanarium? Thank you for your help.

Body: The main part of the letter explains the writer's reason for writing.

Yours truly,
Matthew Langdon

Closing: The letter ends with *Yours truly* or *Sincerely* followed by a comma.

Signature: The writer signs his name in script.

Make a Plan

When you write a business letter, you must have a clear purpose in mind. Your message should be accurate and to the point.

Choose a Reason to Write

Think about reasons why you might write a business letter. Is there information that you need for a report or a vacation trip, or is there something about your school or community that you are concerned about?

- Brainstorm a list of possible topics for writing a business letter.
- Write your ideas on an idea sheet.
- Choose the one that interests you the most.

Choose What You Want to Know, Receive, or Share

Research the company, organization, or official that you need to contact.

- Decide what you would like to receive from the company, organization, or official. Do you want to receive a brochure about a place to visit or a new product? Maybe you want to share your concerns about a school problem or a broken cassette tape. List your ideas on your idea sheet.
- Find out who should get your letter and where it should be sent. Put the name and address on your sheet as well.

Organize Your Writing

Now start planning your letter. This information sheet will help you focus on your purpose for writing.

Product, service, or complaint:_____

Purpose for writing:_____

What you hope to get:_____

Name and title of person:_____

_____

Company name and address:_____

_____

Write It Down

Start Off Right!

You've planned your letter, so now it's time to write your first draft.

- Begin by reviewing the format of business letters.
- Then, neatly write or type your home address and the date about halfway across the page.
- Write the inside address at the left margin.
- Add the salutation. If you don't know the person's name, use *Sir or Madam.* Place a colon at the end of the salutation.

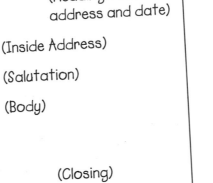

(Heading: return address and date)

(Inside Address)

(Salutation)

(Body)

(Closing)

(Signature)

Tech Tip

Set two tabs for your letter—one at .5 in. for paragraph indents and one at 3.5 in. for the heading and closing.

Keep Your Reader Interested

- Write the body of your letter. In two or three short paragraphs, explain why you are writing and describe what information, product, or result you would like.
- Use formal language and a businesslike tone.

Bring Your Letter to a Close

- Thank the person for helping you.
- End your letter with a closing followed by a comma. Place the closing halfway across the page.
- Put your signature directly below the closing.

Conferencing

Read your business letter aloud to a partner. Does your partner think that the message is clearly stated? Is the tone businesslike and polite?

Portfolio

Keep your idea sheet with your first draft. You may need to send a second letter!

Look It Over

Read your letter from the point of view of the person who will receive it.

- Is your request clear?
- Are the tone and language correct?
- Have you checked that words are correctly spelled, abbreviated, and capitalized and that sentences are correctly punctuated?

If you decide to send your letter, revise, edit, and proofread it carefully. After you have made any needed changes, copy it over in your best handwriting or print out a clean copy. Be sure to sign your name below the closing.

Share Your Work

Business letters can be published in several ways. Here are two suggestions for publishing yours.

Handwritten Letter

If your final handwritten revision is ready to be published, fold it in thirds. Carefully address an envelope (see the model on page 150) and add a stamp in the upper-right corner. Insert your letter with the cut edges to the back of the envelope. Seal the envelope and place it in a nearby mailbox.

E-Mail Letter

Publish your letter by E-mail! Find out if the person, company, or organization you are sending your letter to has an E-mail address. If so, write it carefully on a sheet of paper. Be sure to include any punctuation, special symbols, and capitalized letters. Begin by typing your topic in the "Subject" line, and then add the person's or company's E-mail address in the "To" line. Next, type your letter in the empty message space. Finish by typing your name. Check with your teacher about what personal and address information to include.

Adventures in Writing

Enter the unknown. Step into the world of research, where you can explore a topic that you have always wondered about. Like all explorers, you will probably want to share what you've learned. That's why most research is published in the form of a report. A **research report** tells others what you have learned.

A Research Report

★ **Is a written report about a single topic**

★ **Contains factual information gathered from a variety of sources, such as books, magazines, CD-ROMs, and the Internet**

★ **Gives the information in an easy-to-follow order**

★ **Uses the writer's own words**

★ **Has a clear introduction, body, and conclusion**

★ **Identifies the sources of information used**

Meet the Writer

Writing a research report gave me a chance to tell people about something I've always been interested in. Scientists already know a lot about the sun, and yet there's still more to be discovered.

Frank
Di Biano
New Jersey

Think It Through

When you do research and write a report, you become something of an expert about a topic. You might even hear a classmate say, "Wow, that kid knows everything about ____!" Your first task is to fill in that blank. Everyone is curious about something, so you'll find that choosing a topic for a report is not very hard at all.

Brainstorm and Select a Topic

Brainstorm ideas for your research report. Try looking through your journal, Learning Log, or Observation Log for more ideas. Maybe one of your ideas will turn out to be a good topic, either for you or for a classmate.

Organizing your ideas in a chart with general categories can be helpful.

Frank's Chart

Nature
1. how bees make honey
2. what makes hurricanes
3. world's largest fish

News
1. new treatment for cancer
2. most popular pet

Space
1. the sun
2. first moon flight
3. flights to Mars

Our Community
1. history of town
2. famous people

Ideas for topics are probably playing leapfrog in your head. Now's the time to trap the good ones on paper.

- Make a list of possible topics.
- Next to each idea, jot down notes about why the topic interests you.
- Choose the topic that really appeals to you or makes you curious.

Narrow a Topic

Think about your topic. Is it fairly broad, or is it focused and narrow? If it is too broad, you can narrow it by using an inverted triangle. List the broader topics at the top. Write the narrowed topic at the bottom. See the triangle that Frank made to narrow his topic.

Astronomy

Solar systems

Asteroids, comets, eclipses, planets, meteors, moons, stars

The sun

Use an inverted triangle to narrow your topic.

- Write the general topic in the top part of the triangle.
- Add topics below it that each get a little more narrow.
- Identify the narrow topic you wish to research.

Design a Plan

After Frank narrowed his topic, he thought about what he already knew about the sun and what he wanted to learn. He put his information in a KWL chart. Then, he circled several questions—the ones he really wanted to research.

TOPIC: THE SUN

What I **Know**	What I **Want** to Know	What I **Learned**
1. The sun is a star	What kind of star is it?	
	Why does it fascinate scientists?	
2. It produces heat and light	How is the light made?	
	How hot is the sun?	
	How does heat affect living things?	

Illustration: Sun coming over horizon

Use a KWL chart to help you design your writing plan. Write questions you want to ask. Add notes about what sources you might use to find the answers. Add more questions if they come to mind. Then, circle the questions you really want to find answers to.

Dig Into Your Research

You have prepared a list of questions to guide your research. Now it's time to begin gathering factual information on your topic. A good place to start is the library. Information sources that you can find there include

- books
- encyclopedias
- magazines
- newspapers
- CD-ROMs
- the Internet
- the librarian

Check with your librarian if you're not sure how to find or use some of these research tools.

To find books on your topic, you can use the library's card catalog. The card catalog is a large cabinet with drawers that contain file cards arranged in alphabetical order. These cards list information by title, author, or subject.

535. GH JUV BK	**Let's look at sunshine** **Milburn, Constance** Let's look at sunshine/Constance Milburn; language consultant Diana Bentley; illustrated by Dan Woods and Carolyn Scrace. New York: Hove: Bookwright Press, 1988. 32 p.; col. ill.
	1. Sun

Title Card

Many libraries have an electronic card catalog, too. It lists books by title, author, and subject, and it also lists them by keywords. Keywords are important words or phrases in your topic.

Find... Options... Backup Startover Quit Help...

You searched SUBJECT for: sunlight
SEARCH RESULTS   TITLES 12-17 of 53

1 Wentzel, Donat G., 1934. The restless sun. Washington: Smithsonian Institution Press, 1989.

2 Asimov, Isaac, 1920. The sun. Milwaukee: G. Stevens Pub, 1988.

3 Branley, Franklyn Mansfield, 1915. The sun and the solar systems. 1st. ed. New York: Twenty-First Century Books, 1996.

4 Milburn, Constance, Let's look at sunshine. New York: Hove: Bookwright Press, 1988.

5 Kandoian, Ellen. Under the sun. New York: Dodd, Mead, 1987.

Electronic Subject Search Results

AUTHOR: Milburn, Constance.
TITLE: Let's look at sunshine/Constance Milburn; language consultant Diana Bentley; illustrated by Dan Woods and Carolyn Scrace.

OTHER TITLE: Sunshine.
PUBLISHED: New York: Hove: Bookwright Press, 1988.
PAGING: 32 p.; col. ill.
SERIES: Let's look at

SUBJECTS: Sun.
OTHER ENTRY: Woods, Daniel.
                Scrace, Carolyn.

LCCN: 87-71741
OCLC#: 17811653
ISBN: 0531181782

Electronic Title and Author Card

To find magazine articles, you can search the periodicals index, CD-ROM databases, and some electronic card catalogs. Encyclopedias are in the reference section of the library, on CD-ROMs, or on the Internet. Newspaper articles are on microfiche, CD-ROM databases, and newspapers' web sites.

As you research your topic, look for books and articles that were published recently. These materials are more likely to contain up-to-date information.

You can also use sources that are outside the library. Here are a few.

- Your own experience with the topic
- An interview with an expert
- An Internet search at home or at a friend's house, if you have permission
- Your observations

Now's the time to start your research. Review your questions, and then comb the library's card catalog and other resources to find answers for all of them.

Writer's Tip
Sort your note cards by subtopic and use a rubber band or paper clip to keep them together.

Take Notes

As you read and read lots of interesting facts and details about your topic, it's impossible to remember them all. That's why it is important to take good notes.

There are three types of notes. One is where you record the exact words of an author. The second is where you write short notes. (For help with notes, see page 38.) The third is where you summarize the main points of an article. (See Summaries, on page 44.) Use index cards to record your information.

- Write one fact, quotation, or summary per card.
- Always include the source and page number.
- If you are copying an author's exact words, enclose them in quotation marks.

Summary

Sun, © 1996 Grolier's Multimedia Encyclopedia.
CD-ROM. 1996 ed.

The
sys
It c
864
fusi

Notes

"Sun." Grolier's Multimedia Encyclopedia.
CD-ROM. 1996 ed.
- Nuclear fusion creates the sun's energy

Exact Words

"Sun." Grolier's Multimedia Encyclopedia.
CD-ROM. 1996 ed.
"The sun, the central body of the solar system and the closest star, is an immense sphere of glowing gas."

You've found many resources that contain information about your topic. Now it's time to take notes. Record on index cards the information you think you may want to include in your report. Remember to carefully write your notes and record your sources accurately. Also be sure to use quotation marks to show an author's exact words.

Cite Sources of Information

You may find that your readers want to know more about your topic or something in your report. To find this information, they'd turn to your bibliography. Here's how to create a bibliography.

- Prepare a note card for each source.
- On the card, accurately record the author, title, and all publication information—the place of publication, the publisher, and the date of publication.
- Arrange each card alphabetically by author's last name.
- Write the information in the correct form for bibliographies. (See Frank's final model on page 175.)

Here are two of Frank's note cards. Notice how he followed the proper form for a bibliographic entry.

> Milburn, Constance
> Let's Look at Sunshine
> New York: Hove: Bookwright Press, 1988

> Observer's Handbook
> Toronto, Canada: Royal Astronomical
> Society of Canada (yearly)

Portfolio

Store your note cards and questions. You will refer to these at each stage of writing your research report.

Make an Outline

Now you need to organize your information. Making an outline can help you order your facts and ideas.

Here is Frank's outline.

The Sun

I.   Introduction
II. Why the sun is important
     A. Gives light to planets in solar system
     B. Earth depends on sun to grow plants
     C. Living things would die without light
III. What the sun is
     A. A star
     B. Largest object in solar system
     C. Mostly hydrogen gas
     D. Extremely hot
IV. Structure of the sun
     A. Photosphere
     B. Chromosphere and spicules
     C. Corona
     D. Core
V.   Conclusion

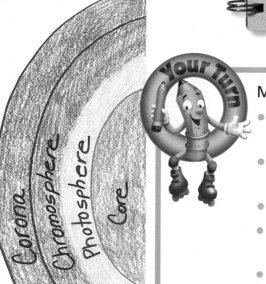

Make an outline to use when you write.

- Look over your notes and circle the most important facts and ideas about your topic.
- List these main ideas in an order that makes sense. Leave a few lines between each.
- Number the main ideas with Roman numerals.
- Under each main idea, write two or three details. Include only the details you will use in your report.
- Use capital letters to order the details.

Conferencing

Talk with a partner. Is your topic narrow enough? Does the order of your outline make sense? Do your details relate to your main ideas? Does your partner have other questions that might help you?

Put It Into Words

While doing the research for his report, Frank learned a lot about the sun. Here's the first page of his two-page report. Did Frank stick to his outline? Is there any information that he forgot to include?

The sun: An Important Star
by Frank Di Biano

What is made up mostly of hydrogen, is very wide, and has several different layers? It's also very old—about 5,000,000,000 years old! If you guessed the sun, you're right! The sun was studied by ancient peoples and scientists and still interests researchers today.

The sun is a star and a very important one. It provides sunlight to all the planets in our soler system. Earth depends on the sun's light to grow plants. If the sun stops shining, nothing would grow. Then, animals would not have plants to eat eventually there would be no living things on our planet at all. Earth would become a dark, cold place if the sun stopped producing light.

Scientists believe there is no life on the other planets in our solar system. They think this is true because the planets are either too close to the sun and too hot to grow living things, or they are too far away from the sun and too cold to grow living things.

The sun is like many other stars in our galaxy. Other galaxies near us are the Milky Way and Andromeda. The sun is just a medium-sized star. It is the biggest object in our soler system.

> **The introduction gets the reader's attention.**

> **Facts are used to keep the reader interested.**

> **Each paragraph presents a different main idea.**

Photo: Solar flares

Here is the second page of Frank's report. Frank continued to follow his outline as he wrote. Notice how he summarized his research in the conclusion.

The supporting sentences in a paragraph give more information and facts.

Scientists say that it is a large mass of hydrogen and other gases and is about 864,000 miles in diameter, or width. The temperature in the middle of the sun is 29,000,000°F. Natural nuclear energy creates the light and heat that come from the sun.

The structure of the sun has fascinated scientists for centuries. The photosphere is the layer we can see. Scientists have discovered that the sun has many layers. It is about 300 miles thick.

The language is formal.

The layer above the photosphere is called the chromosphere. Sticking through the chromosphere are spicules, which are streaming jets of gas. Beyond the chromosphere is the corona. The corona is the sun's thin, hot outer atmosphere.

The writer uses his own words.

On the inside of the sun, the pressure, temperature, and density increase. Density is how much something weighs compared to how much space it takes up. The outer part of the sun is like boiling

The writer uses an analogy to explain something new.

water that forces the energy inside the sun to the surface. The core is extremely hot because of this pressure.

The conclusion sums up the main ideas.

The sun makes life possible on Earth because of the light it provides. It is an important and fascinating star that never ceases to amaze scientists and observers alike.

Here is Frank's bibliography. He used information from nine different sources. Each source is listed by the author's last name or the book or article title if there is no identified author.

Bibliography

Greeley, Ronald, and Raymond Batson. <u>The NASA atlas of the Solar System.</u> New York: Cambridge University Press, 1996.

Beatty, J. Kelly, Brian O'Leary, and Andrew Chaiken, eds. <u>The New Solar System.</u> 2nd ed. Cambridge, MA: Sky Publishing Corp., 1982.

Branley, Franklyn Mansfield. <u>The sun and the Solar System.</u> New York: Twenty-First Century Books, 1996.

Hoyt, Douglas V., and Kenneth H. Shatten. <u>The Role of the Sun in Climate Change.</u> New York: Oxford University Press, 1997.

Milburn, Constance. <u>Let's Look at Sunshine.</u> New York: Hove: Bookwright Press, 1988.

<u>Observer's Handbook.</u> Toronto, Canada: Royal Astronomical Society of Canada (yearly).

"Sun." <u>Grolier's Multimedia Encyclopedia.</u> CD-ROM. Danbury, CT: Grolier Electronic Publishing, Inc., 1996.

"Sun." <u>Webster's New World Encyclopedia.</u> New York: Prentice Hall General Reference, 1992.

Zim, Herbert S., Robert H. Baker, and Mark R. Chartrand. <u>Stars,</u> rev. ed. New York: Golden Press, 1985.

The bibliography goes on a separate page at the end.

Editors' names are used as the names of authors.

The city where published, the publisher's name, and the date of publication are given.

Book titles are underlined if written by hand or italicized if printed on a computer.

Sources are listed in alphabetical order by last name or article title.

With two or more authors, the first author's last name is written first.

Photo: The sun rising over Earth, as seen from space shuttle

As you write your research report, ask yourself

★ **Subject:** What is my topic and what is the best way to introduce it?

★ **Audience:** Who will be reading my report?

★ **Purpose:** How can I make my report interesting, informative, and clear?

★ **Form:** Have I followed the format for a research report?

Writer's Tip
Reports often use special or technical words. Don't worry about spelling these unusual words. Mistakes will be fixed later.

Your Turn

Now it's time to write a draft of your research report. Review your information. Then, follow your outline. Remember to write the report in your own words, using formal language. Concentrate on getting all your ideas down on paper. Use the Drafting Checklist as a guide.

Drafting Checklist
- An interesting topic sentence introduces your subject.
- The first main idea in the body is given, and then details about it are added.
- Each new paragraph begins with a new main idea. A paragraph with a lot of details is divided into two or more paragraphs.
- The report ends with a summary of the facts and your final thoughts or conclusions.
- Your bibliography lists your sources.
- The report keeps the reader involved.
- The outline was followed.
- Formal language is used.

Portfolio
Save your draft and keep it with your outline and notes. You will need these items when you revise your report.

Tech Tip
Double-space and use wide margins so that you will have room on the printout to write notes and corrections.

Conferencing
Read your draft to a partner. Ask if your information is well organized. What suggestions does your partner have for improving your report?

Take Another Look

When Frank reread his draft, he realized that he needed to include more ideas and details. He reviewed his outline. Then, he added more information to the first page of his research report.

The sun: An Important Star
by Frank Di Biano

What is made up mostly of hydrogen, is very wide, and has several different layers? It's also very old—about 5,000,000,000 years old! If you guessed the sun, you're right! The sun was studied by ancient peoples and scientists and still interests researchers today.

The sun is a star and a very important one. It provides sunlight to all the planets in our soler system. Earth depends on the sun's light to grow plants. If the sun stops shining, nothing would grow. Then, animals would not have plants to eat eventually there would be no living things on our planet at all. Earth would become a dark, cold place if the sun stopped producing light.

Scientists believe there is no life on the other planets in our solar system. They think this is true because the planets are either too close to the sun and too hot to grow living things, or they are too far away from the sun and too cold to grow living things.

The planets closest to earth, for example, are Mars and Venus. Mars is the first planet beyond Earth, but its temperature is too cold for plant or animal life. It can be as cold as -199°F there. Venus, which is one planet closer to the sun from earth, is about 900°F on the surface of the planet. It is too hot. Neither planet can support animal or plant life.

Insert information and examples that had been left out.

Photo: Earth, just before sunrise, as seen from space shuttle.

Here are more revisions that Frank made to this part
of his report. How do they improve his writing?

Delete unimportant information.

The sun is like many other stars in our galaxy. ~~Other galaxies near us are the Milky Way and Andromeda.~~ The sun is just a medium-sized star. It is the biggest object in our soler system. Scientists say that it is a large mass of hydrogen and other gases

Add important information.

and is about 864,000 miles in diameter, or width. The temperature in
almost 16,000,000° on the Kelvin scale, or about
the middle of the sun is 29,000,000°F. Natural nuclear energy
creates the light and heat that come from the sun.

The structure of the sun has fascinated scientists for centuries.

Move a sentence to improve order of ideas.

The photosphere is the layer we can see. Scientists have discovered that the sun has many layers. It is about 300 miles thick.

Add new information.

Because the temperature in the photosphere
is so hot, the sun looks like it's yellow.
The layer above the photosphere is called the chromosphere.

Sticking through the chromosphere are spicules, which are streaming

Add another important detail.

jets of gas. Beyond the chromosphere is the corona. The corona is
It reaches at least 1,000,000 miles out into space.
the sun's thin, hot outer atmosphere.

On the inside of the sun, the pressure, temperature, and density increase. Density is how much something weighs compared to how much space it takes up. The outer part of the sun is like boiling

Add more important information.

water that forces the energy inside the sun to the surface.
, which is only a small part of the sun,
The core is extremely hot because of this pressure.

Photo: Sunrise, as seen from space station *Mir*

Now it's time to revise your research report. Look at it with a fresh eye. Did you include all the important facts you need? Is there information that's not really related to your topic that you can delete? Does your conclusion sum up the most important ideas? Use this Revising Checklist to help you improve your draft.

Revising Marks

≡	capitalize
∧	add
✄	remove
⊙	add a period
/	make lowercase
◡	move
∼	transpose

Revising Checklist

- Does the report use formal language and sound like it was written in my own words?
- Does each paragraph have a topic sentence that sounds interesting?
- Is my report easy to follow?
- Does any part of my report seem out of order?
- Do all the facts relate to the topic? Is there anything that could be cut?
- Does the end sum up the facts and give my final thoughts?

Conferencing

Read your report to a classmate or classmates. What do they like about your report? What can be made better? Go through the Revising Checklist questions and take notes as you consider your classmates' suggestions.

Tech Tip
Save each draft as a new file. Add labels, like *Draft 1* or *Draft 2*, so that you can tell which is which.

Portfolio
Save your revisions, drafts, and notes until you are ready to edit and proofread your writing.

Become a Super Writer

Examples can add much detail, interest, and variety to your research report. For help in using examples, see the *Writer's Handbook* section, page 223.

Polish Your Writing

Frank was pleased with the way his research report turned out. He knew that he probably overlooked some mistakes, so he was extra careful when he edited and proofread his work. See what he corrected on this page of his report.

Capitalize an important word in the title.

Correct a spelling error.

Change a verb to the correct tense.

Fix a run-on sentence.

Capitalize a proper noun.

The sun: An Important Star
By Frank Di Biano

What is made up mostly of hydrogen, is very wide, and has several different layers? It's also very old—about 5,000,000,000 years old! If you guessed the sun, you're right! The sun was studied by ancient peoples and scientists and still interests researchers today.

The sun is a star and a very important one. It provides sunlight to
solar
all the planets in our ~~soler~~ system. Earth depends on the sun's light to
stopped
grow plants. If the sun ~~stops~~ shining, nothing would grow. Then,
, and
animals would not have plants to eat eventually there would be no living things on our planet at all. Earth would become a dark, cold place if the sun stopped producing light.

Scientists believe there is no life on the other planets in our solar system. They think this is true because the planets are either too close to the sun and too hot to grow living things, or they are too far away from the sun and too cold to grow living things. The planets closest to earth, for example, are Mars and Venus. Mars is the first planet beyond Earth, but its temperature is too cold for plant or animal life. It can be as cold as −199°F there.

This part of Frank's report has more corrections. How do you think they improve his writing?

Capitalize a proper noun.

Replace a noun with a pronoun.

Fix a spelling error.

Combine two sentences.

Replace a noun with a pronoun.

Venus, which is one planet closer to the sun from earth, is about 900°F on the surface of the planet. It is too hot. Neither planet can support animal or plant life.

The sun is like many other stars in our galaxy. The sun *It* is just a medium-sized star, *but* It is the biggest object in our soler *solar* system. Scientists say that it is a large mass of hydrogen and other gases and is about 864,000 miles in diameter, or width. The temperature in the middle of the sun is almost 16,000,000° on the Kelvin scale, or about 29,000,000°F. Natural nuclear energy creates the light and heat that come from the sun.

The structure of the sun has fascinated scientists for centuries. *They* Scientists have discovered that the sun has many layers. The photosphere is the layer we can see. It is about 300 miles thick. Because the temperature in the photosphere is so hot, the sun looks like it's yellow.

The layer around the photosphere is called the chromosphere. Sticking through the chromosphere are spicules, which are streaming jets of gas. Beyond the chromosphere is the corona. The corona is the sun's thin, hot outer atmosphere. It reaches at least 1,000,000 miles out into space.

Photo: *Skylab* ultraviolet photo of solar eruption

Proofreading Marks

¶	indent first line of paragraph
≡	capitalize
∧ or ∨	add
✗	remove
⊙	add a period
/	make lowercase
◯	spelling mistake
∽	move
∾	transpose

As you read your report, pretend that you've never seen it before. Look for spelling, punctuation, capitalization, and grammar mistakes. Use proofreading marks to show your changes. The Editing and Proofreading Checklist can help you polish your writing.

Tech Tip

For a long report, use the Page Up and Page Down commands to get from the top of one page to the top of another.

Editing and Proofreading Checklist

- Are there any sentences that I can combine?

  See page 246 in the *Writer's Handbook* section.

- Do my verbs change tense?

  See page 252 in the *Writer's Handbook* section.

- Have I capitalized proper nouns, titles of people, and place names correctly?

  See page 266 in the *Writer's Handbook* section.

- Did I use italics and underlining correctly?

  See page 272 in the *Writer's Handbook* section.

- Did I spell all the words correctly?

  See pages 275–284 in the *Writer's Handbook* section.

Portfolio

Keep your final draft together with all your notes and your outline until you are ready to publish.

Conferencing

Ask your partner to carefully read your report. Can your partner find any mistakes that you missed? If so, talk about ways to fix the errors. Mark your corrections on your draft.

Become a Super Writer

Citations are important to researchers. To be sure you are citing your sources correctly, see page 268 in the *Writer's Handbook* section.

Share Your Work

Frank decided to publish his report by giving an oral presentation. He printed out his report, and then his teacher made an overhead transparency for each page. Here is the first page of Frank's report.

The Sun: An Important and Fascinating Star
by Frank Di Biano

What is made up mostly of hydrogen, is very wide, and has several different layers? It's also very old—about 5,000,000,000 years old! If you guessed the sun, you're right! The sun was studied by ancient peoples and scientists and still interests researchers today.

The sun is a star and a very important one. It provides sunlight to all the planets in our solar system. Earth depends on the sun's light to grow plants. If the sun stopped shining, nothing would grow. Then, animals would not have plants to eat, and eventually there would be no living things on our planet at all. Earth would become a dark, cold place if the sun stopped producing light.

Scientists believe there is no life on the other planets in our solar system. They think this is true because the planets are either too close to the sun and too hot to grow living things, or they are too far away from the sun and too cold to grow living things. The planets closest to Earth, for example, are Mars and Venus. Mars is the first planet beyond Earth, but its temperature is too cold for plant or animal life. It can be as cold as -199°F there. Venus, which is one planet closer to the sun from Earth, is about 900°F on the surface of the planet. It is too hot. Neither planet can support animal or plant life.

Here is the second page of Frank's research report. Do you think Frank included the right amount of interesting information in his report? Read on and decide for yourself.

°F (in millions)

The sun is like many other stars in our galaxy. It is just a medium-sized star, but it is the biggest object in our solar system. Scientists say that it is a large mass of hydrogen and other gases and is about 864,000 miles in diameter, or width. The temperature in the middle of the sun is almost 16,000,000° on the Kelvin scale, or about 29,000,000°F. Natural nuclear energy creates the light and heat that come from the sun.

The structure of the sun has fascinated scientists for centuries. They have discovered that the sun has many layers. The photosphere is the layer we can see. It is about 300 miles thick. Because the temperature in the photosphere is so hot, the sun looks like it's yellow.

The layer above the photosphere is called the chromosphere. Sticking through the chromosphere are spicules, which are streaming jets of gas. Beyond the chromosphere is the corona. The corona is the sun's thin, hot outer atmosphere. It reaches at least 1,000,000 miles out into space.

On the inside of the sun, the pressure, temperature, and density increase. Density is how much something weighs compared to how much space it takes up. The outer part of the sun is like boiling water that forces the energy inside the sun to the surface. The core, which is only a small part of the sun, is extremely hot because of this pressure.

The sun makes life possible on Earth because of the light it provides. It is an important and fascinating star that never ceases to amaze scientists and observers alike.

This is Frank's final bibliography, which he included on the last page of his research report. Notice the corrections he made to it.

Bibliography

Beatty, J. Kelly, Brian O'Leary, and Andrew Chaiken, eds. *The New Solar System*. 2nd ed. Cambridge, MA: Sky Publishing Corp., 1982.

Branley, Franklyn Mansfield. *The Sun and the Solar System*. New York: Twenty-First Century Books, 1996.

Greeley, Ronald, and Raymond Batson. *The NASA Atlas of the Solar System*. New York: Cambridge University Press, 1996.

Hoyt, Douglas V., and Kenneth H. Shatten. *The Role of the Sun in Climate Change*. New York: Oxford University Press, 1997.

Milburn, Constance. *Let's Look at Sunshine*. New York: Hove: Bookwright Press, 1988.

Observer's Handbook. Toronto, Canada: Royal Astronomical Society of Canada (yearly).

"Sun." *Grolier's Multimedia Encyclopedia*. CD-ROM. Danbury, CT: Grolier Electronic Publishing, Inc., 1996.

"Sun." *Webster's New World Encyclopedia*. New York: Prentice Hall General Reference, 1992.

Zim, Herbert S., Robert H. Baker, and Mark R. Chartrand. *Stars*. Rev. ed. New York: Golden Press, 1985.

Capitalized an important word in a book's title.

Moved an entry to fit alphabetically.

Illustration: The Solar System as seen looking toward Earth from the moon

Here are some suggestions for ways to publish your report.

Be a Guest Expert ▶

Present your report to the class as a "guest speaker." Afterward, hold a question-and-answer period. Remember, you are an expert on your topic. Share the interesting facts you learned.

◀ Class Encyclopedia

Publish a class encyclopedia. Add illustrations, photographs, and charts, and then arrange the reports alphabetically by topic. Give a copy to your school library so everyone can learn from your research.

Create a Multimedia Presentation ▶

Use presentation or slide show software to present your research report. Select information and photos to include on each slide. Ask your teacher for good Internet sites for photos. When done, check that your slide show works well. As you present your report, ask a partner to use sign language to sign any spoken words or sounds that you included in your slide show.

Cyber Encyclopedia

Submit your research report to *Kidopedia*—a children's encyclopedia on the Internet written by kids:
www.kidlib.org/kidopedia/

Writing a Problem-Solution Essay

Have you ever heard the saying "For every problem there is a solution"? Even if this saying isn't quite true, there are plenty of problems that do have solutions. One way to approach a problem is to identify its cause, come up with some solutions, and pick the best solution. In fact, that's your goal when you write a **problem-solution essay.**

Jennifer's goal in her problem-solution essay was to solve the problem of not having enough money for the holidays. This is a problem you may face sometime, too. Jennifer has lots of ideas. See what you think of them.

Raking It In

by Jennifer Miller

> **The writer grabs the reader's attention in the first sentence.**

After counting your current cash stash, are you feeling a bit crunched? That spare change in your piggy bank just won't cut it when buying presents for the holidays— just around the bend. You can't get a "real job" (or drive yourself there). Yet, you can build up your cash flow if you get creative.

> **A believable problem is introduced, and a goal is set.**

But first, let's start with some considerations to think over.

- Decide how much money you need. Are you buying a few select gifts or a billion teeny gifts for every friend since nursery school?

- Think your idea through instead of assuming you can sell anything. People won't pay for a service just because you're adorable. People pay for what they need or strongly want.

- Everyone loves your bracelets, but they're not going to fly if half the school is selling them. Make sure your service or product is unique.

> **The writer uses a linking verb to tell more about a noun.**

- Ask friends to tell others about your service. Don't be shy!

- Jobs you can start tomorrow . . .

> **The writer uses bullets to highlight each consideration.**

1. Take on extra chores.

Ask your folks if they'd be willing to shell out extra bucks if you add jobs to your chore list: dusting, vacuuming, sweeping, watering plants, whatever.

2. Start a card-making service.

Make custom holiday greetings. Head to a craft store for paper in bulk, plus decorations to spruce them up (ink pads, stencils, glitter, stickers).

3. Offer a gift-wrapping service.

Make a bunch of flyers letting neighbors know what services you can offer to make their lives easier. Offer to decorate, wrap presents, address and seal holiday cards. List your fees, and include your name and number.

4. Baby-sit.

Bring along a bag of toys and games. Tots love to play with something new, and seeing the goodie bag will help them say goodbye to Mommy and Daddy a lot more easily.

5. Be a party helper.

Throwing parties can be overwhelming. Many moms would love to find someone to help out by bringing baked goods, entertaining kids, decorating the house, and cleaning up afterward.

6. Put on a show.

Here's a good way to start your path to Broadway. Write a play or comedy routine, and then perform it for $1 admission price. Serve popcorn and drinks to make even more extra money.

7. Make jewelry.

Teach yourself the ins and outs of jewelry making, and sell your products to friends and family. Hey, they're looking for inexpensive holiday gifts to give, too!

No solution is singled out as the best solution.

8. Hold a car wash.

Depending on what region of the country you live in, this idea may send chills up your spine—but cars get dirty in cold weather, too. Dress warmly, then throw on your most waterproof coat and boots, and get spraying.

Talk About the Model

As a Reader

★ What problem does the writer identify? What is its cause?

★ Do you feel that this problem could be important to you, too?

★ Which solution appeals the most to you? Why?

As a Writer

★ How does the writer grab the reader's interest at the beginning?

★ How does the writer make you feel that she is a good friend of yours?

★ Where do you think the writer got her ideas for the solutions?

★ Why do you think the writer uses bullets and numbered lists instead of paragraphs?

★ The author didn't choose a best solution at the end. Why do you think she didn't?

Make a Plan

Before you can write your problem-solution essay, you need to decide on a problem and make a plan.

Pick a Problem

What problem do you want to write about? Can you think of any problems that other kids your age might have? Brainstorm a list of problems about school, your community, making friends, or whatever. Choose the one that your readers may be able to relate to in some way.

Organize Causes and Solutions

Make a chart that identifies the problem and tells why it's a problem. Brainstorm possible solutions for the problem. Write these ideas in the chart.

Problem:

  Causes:

    1.

    2.

  Possible solutions:

    1.

    2.

    3.

    4.

    5.

    6.

Try Out Your Solutions

Find out if your solutions work.

- Try out each solution, if possible.
- If you can't test a specific solution, perhaps there are classmates who have already tried it. Think of who these students might be. Then, interview them to find out if the solution worked.
- The solutions that work are the ones to use when you write your essay.

Sometimes you can help your readers by identifying the solution that you think works best. Think about the problem you are writing about and decide if this is true for it.

Write It Down

As you write your problem-solution essay, remember that you are writing to inform your readers. Think about who your audience is and the kind of language and tone you should use for your audience.

Identify the Problem

Choose a way to begin that states your topic and catches your reader's attention.

- Start by describing the problem or by providing an example or two of the problem.
- Explain why you think it's a problem and identify the problem's causes.
- Tell why you have chosen this problem.

Present the Solutions

Stay focused on the problem throughout your essay. Use your chart as a guide.

- Present your possible solutions.
- Describe each solution precisely and explain how it can solve the problem. Use a new paragraph or list to write about each solution.
- Use linking verbs to tell more about the subjects of sentences.

Wrap It Up

Write your conclusion.

- Summarize the problem.
- Offer your thoughts about the best way to solve the problem—if this works for your topic.
- Explain why you think your solution or solutions really tackle the problem.

Conferencing

Read your problem-solution essay to a partner or group of classmates. Ask if your essay targets the problem and presents realistic solutions. Do your partners agree that you should recommend one solution or many different solutions?

Tech Tip
Use boldface, italics, or underlining for emphasis.

Portfolio

Store your handwritten and printed notes, charts, and drafts, plus your disk of computer files.

Look It Over

Tech Tip
Use bullets to mark special lists and words.

Reread your essay. Are there any changes you want to make? Did you identify the problem clearly and describe its causes and possible solutions? Did you use linking verbs correctly? Set your essay aside and revise it later if you wish. Remember to check that your grammar, usage, mechanics, and spelling are all correct.

Share Your Work

After you've revised, edited, and proofread your writing, pick a way to publish it.

Publish a Class Magazine

Have classmates share their problem-solution essays in a class magazine. Design an appealing cover, and add illustrations, photographs, and charts to accompany the essays. Make color or black-and-white copies, and then pass them out to other students and give one to the school library.

Live on TV

Present a live program for your classmates.

- Pretend to be an interviewed guest on a TV news-and-entertainment show.
- Recruit a classmate to be your interviewer.
- Copy your problem-solution essay onto index cards, listing one solution per card.
- Have your interviewer ask you questions about your topic.
- Refer to your note cards if needed.
- Perhaps your classmates could ask additional questions about your topic.

Share With Kids Around the World

Type a clean final copy of your problem-solution essay. Have your teacher review it. Then, send the essay to one of the following sites to have it published with other children's writing on the Internet. Check with your teacher for more sites.

KidPub, at **Submissions@KidPub.org**

Children's Express, at **www.ce.org/interact/onr.htm**

IN MY OPINION

Writing to Persuade

Writing a Persuasive Paragraph

Meet the Writer

"Waste not, want not" is a saying I learned from my grandmother. To me, wasting water is wrong.

Carolyn Reimers
Minnesota

Words are powerful. If you put your words together in the right way, you can convince people to share your view. When you write to prove a point or defend an opinion, you are writing to persuade. In this **persuasive paragraph,** the writer tells why everyone should save water.

Down the Drain
by Carolyn Reimers

People who waste water are big drips! Every time you leave the water running in the sink, you waste gallons of water. Don't wait until a drought happens before saving water. Use water wisely NOW. For example, if you turn off the water while you brush your teeth, you save 10 gallons a day. If you fix a leaky faucet, you save 100 gallons a day. Use a broom instead of the hose to clean the sidewalk. Don't use the dishwasher or washing machine until you have a full load. If we all save water, we will have water when we really need it. Don't be a big drip. Start saving water now!

Talk About the Model

★ How does the writer get your attention?

★ What does the writer want you to do?

★ What is the writer's best argument? Why?

Make a Plan

Now it's your turn to make a plan.

- First, quick write to list some topics that you know people disagree about.

- Choose a topic that you feel strongly about.

- Brainstorm ideas about that topic. Use a cluster diagram like Carolyn's to organize your thoughts.

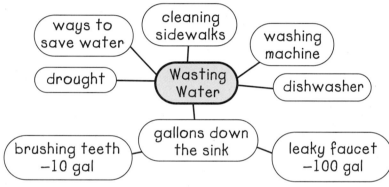

ways to save water

cleaning sidewalks

washing machine

drought

Wasting Water

dishwasher

brushing teeth −10 gal

gallons down the sink

leaky faucet −100 gal

Tech Tip

Use the Tab key to indent paragraphs. View your paragraph in Document Layout form to check your margins.

Write It Down

- Start with a topic sentence. State your subject and what you want readers to believe or do.

- Support your opinion. Give at least three reasons and examples. Save your best reason for last.

- End by summarizing your ideas. Then, ask readers to agree with you and take action.

Portfolio

Store the notes and drafts for your persuasive paragraph in case you decide to revise, edit, and publish it.

Conferencing

Read your paragraph to a partner. Ask if your reasons are clear and convincing. Does your partner have other suggestions to consider?

Look It Over

Read your paragraph carefully. Did you state reasons and give examples to convince the reader to agree with you? Check for mistakes in grammar and spelling.

Writing an Editorial Article

What do you think? Does your community need a new park? Should there be a curfew for people under 18? These are issues on which people take sides. Newspapers and other opinion makers also take sides on issues. They express their opinions in **editorial articles**. In this editorial, the writer presents a strong case for "using your head."

TexasMedical Association

The main problem is stated in the first paragraph.

Examples show why the problem is important.

A solution is suggested.

Use Your Head When Riding a Bike

Bicycles are seen by many people as toys for children or exercise equipment for adults. Without proper protection, however, bicycles can be dangerous or even deadly.

Each year in the United States, an estimated 1,000 people die from bicycle-related crashes. Of those deaths, 62 percent are caused by head injuries. Thousands of young bike riders are treated in emergency departments each year for head trauma; of the 500 children who die each year riding bikes, 80 percent are victims of head trauma.

Most of these tragedies can be prevented by the addition of one simple piece of equipment: a bicycle helmet. The likelihood of head injury is reduced by about 85 percent by using a bike helmet. In fact, universal use of bike helmets could save one life every day and prevent one head injury every four minutes.

Talk About the Model

As a Reader

★ What does the editorial want readers to do?

★ Did the editorial convince you? Why or why not?

As a Writer

★ What is the best reason or example the writers used?

★ Who is the audience for this editorial? How can you tell?

★ Why would a medical association want to publish this editorial?

Given these statistics, why don't more adults and children wear bike helmets? Some people find them too heavy and uncomfortable, and they may be viewed as too expensive. Especially for children, wearing a bike helmet is not the "cool" thing to do. . . .

Once you have the helmet, getting your child to wear it may be a different challenge. Insist that children wear a helmet any time they ride a bike. Accidents can happen on sidewalks or bike trails as well as streets. Start the helmet habit at a young age: Children who receive a helmet with their first bicycle may view wearing the helmet as a natural habit. Finally, if you ride a bicycle alone or with your child, always wear a helmet yourself. If your helmet is damaged in an accident or any other way, you should replace it, even if the damage isn't obvious.

© 1995 by Texas Medical Association

Formal language is used.

An opposing view is presented.

The writer uses clear, precise sentences.

The writer shows how to take action.

Make a Plan

To get started, plan your editorial article.

Pick Your Topic

Choose an issue that is important to you. It can be a topic that is being debated by people you know, or it might be something you wrote in your Observation Log or journal.

Identify Your Reasons

Next, think about reasons and examples that would convince others to agree with you. List an example for each reason you think of.

Organize Your Writing

A chart like this one can help you prepare your case.

Topic:

My opinion:

Reason 1:   Example:

Reason 2:   Example:

Reason 3:   Example:

Tech Tip

Use a large type size to make the title of your editorial look like a real headline.

Portfolio

If you have organized your portfolio by type of writing, put your editorial article in the Writing to Persuade Section.

Write It Down

- Use clear, precise sentences and formal language in your editorial article.
- In the first paragraph, tell what your topic is. Give your opinion about it.
- Back up your opinion with facts and examples. Use a different paragraph for each reason.
- In the last paragraph, summarize your opinion. Then, ask readers to support you and take action.

Conferencing

Read your editorial to a partner. Ask if you stay focused on your topic. Are your reasons clear and convincing?

Look It Over

Reread your editorial. Is there information you can add or delete? Are negatives used correctly? How are your capitalization and punctuation? Revise, edit, and proofread your editorial if you decide to publish it.

If You Ask Me...

Do you have a favorite book or movie you always recommend to people? A great way to share opinions is to write a **review**. In a review, the writer describes a book, movie, song, or another creative work and lets readers know what he or she liked, didn't like, and why.

A Movie Review

★ Offers an opinion about a movie
★ Is written from the first-person point of view
★ Describes the main characters and events
★ Talks about the movie's good and bad points
★ Backs up the opinion with reasons, details, and examples
★ Answers the question, "Who might enjoy this movie?"

Meet the Writer

I rented this movie for my birthday party. My friends all laughed so hard, it hurt!

Lloyd Williams
Alabama

Think It Through

People read reviews to learn about movies, books, and music they might enjoy. When you write a movie review, you first choose a movie you have seen. Then, you decide what you want to say about it.

Brainstorming

What movies really stick in your brain? Are you a fan of *Aladdin, Star Wars, Titanic, Home Alone, E.T., Ghostbusters, The Sound of Music, Babe, Flubber,* or *Hercules?* What movies do you enjoy seeing over and over? Is there a movie you saw just once but knew right away that you didn't like?

Make a list of the most memorable movies you have seen. Organize your list by types of movies, such as comedies, musicals, cartoons, sci-fi, and action-adventure.

Lloyd's List

ACTION AND ADVENTURE

Indiana Jones
Raiders of the Lost Ark
Men in Black
Goldeneye

COMEDIES

Honey, I Shrunk the Kids
Mrs. Doubtfire
Ace Ventura, Pet Detective
Dr. Dolittle

SCI-FI

Star Trek
Return of the Jedi
Jurassic Park
Batman and Robin

Select a Topic

Decide which movie you want to review. Be sure to pick one that you know well or that you can view at home on videotape if needed.

Design a Plan

Lloyd chose to review *Mrs. Doubtfire*. To get organized, he wrote down what readers would probably want to know about it.

Lloyd's Plan

- MAIN CHARACTERS
  Father/Mrs. Doubtfire, mother, kids, mother's boyfriend.

- MAIN EVENTS
  Robin Williams dresses up as an older grandmother-type of lady and gets a job caring for his kids. He gets jealous of the boyfriend. He switches roles and costumes back and forth in the restaurant.

- WHY I LIKED IT
  It was awesome to see Williams act the part of an older lady.

- WHAT I DIDN'T LIKE, AND WHY
  It isn't believable that his family wouldn't know him or recognize him.

- WHO WOULD LIKE TO SEE THE MOVIE?
  Anyone who likes funny movies.

Your Turn

Now, make your own writing plan. Use Lloyd's list as a guide.

- Remember that you'll be writing from the first-person point of view.
- Start with the basic facts, such as naming the main characters and events in the story.
- Give your opinions and recommendations.
- Be sure to include your reasons for your opinions and recommendations.

Conferencing

Meet with a classmate and review your plan. Have you included enough facts about the movie? Is your opinion clearly stated? Is your opinion supported with reasons and details?

Writer's Tip
To refresh your memory, you might want to look at the movie just before you make your plan.

Portfolio

Store your notes and plan. You will need them when you draft your review.

Put It Into Words

Lloyd selected *Mrs. Doubtfire*, because he thought other people would enjoy the movie. Here is his first draft. Would this movie make you laugh, too?

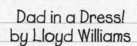

Dad in a Dress!
by Lloyd Williams

The review begins with the title of the movie and the name of its star.

Mrs. Doubtfire is a wacky movie starring Robin Williams. He is a man who dresses up as a lady. When he gets divorced, he hardly ever gets to see his kids. His kids don't recognize him. He wears a wig and a dress and has a funny voice. It isn't very believable, but it makes for one strange scene after another.

The movie's main events are described.

The writer states his opinion of the movie.

As a dad, he was a flake when he is Mrs. Doubtfire, he (or she?) is perfect. He's a great combo of funny and strict. He dances with the vacuum cleaner, and he makes the kids do their homework. After a while, they figure out who he is. They don't tell their mom, though. They love having him around!

Interesting details from the movie are presented.

The most important scenes are discussed.

The funniest scene is in a restaurant. He has to have dinner as himself and at another table as the nanny. He runs to the rest room to switch back and forth. Another time, he orders fancy take-out food and pretends he cooked it.

The writer sums up what he liked about the movie and gives a recommendation.

Mrs. Doubtfire was a huge hit. It is funny. I recommend this movie to anybody!

Think Like a Writer

As you write your first draft, ask yourself

★ **Subject:** Who are the main and supporting characters? What is the movie about?

★ **Audience:** Who will read my review?

★ **Purpose:** How can I help my readers decide whether this movie is for them?

★ **Form:** What are the characteristics of a review? Am I following the correct form?

Now it's time to write your movie review. Read through your notes, follow your plan, and write down all your thoughts. Remember, your purpose is to convince your readers about why they would or would not like to see the movie you're writing about. Use the Drafting Checklist as a guide.

Drafting Checklist

- BEGINNING: Introduce the movie you are reviewing. Give the title and the main characters. In one or two sentences, tell what the movie is about. Explain what makes the movie different from others you've seen.
- MIDDLE: Describe important scenes. Be brief, but use vivid details. Point out what you liked and didn't like, and explain why.
- END: Wrap up your review by suggesting who else might like to see—or not see—this movie.

Conferencing

Share your review with a classmate. Does it convince your partner that your opinion is believable? Did you include enough details to support your opinion?

Writer's Tip
Don't worry about mistakes when you write your first draft. Just aim to get all your thoughts down on paper.

Tech Tip
Instead of underlining the titles of movies and books, put them in italics.

Portfolio
When you store your review, put the first draft at the top of the pile.

Take Another Look

Lloyd's partner asked questions that made Lloyd want to revise his writing to make it clearer in some places. He also thought the end could be better. What changes did Lloyd make? How do you think they made his review better?

Dad in a Dress!
by Lloyd Williams

Mrs. Doubtfire is a wacky movie starring Robin Williams. He is

Add a detail about the plot.

a man who dresses up as a lady. When he gets divorced, he hardly

He misses them so he dresses up as a grandmother
type and gets hired as their nanny.

Rewrite one sentence as two to make the writing clearer.

ever gets to see his kids. His kids don't recognize him. He wears a
○ He also uses
wig and a dress ~~and has~~ a funny voice. It isn't very believable, but

it makes for one strange scene after another.

Delete words to improve the writing.

As a dad, he was a flake when he is Mrs. Doubtfire, he (or

she?) is perfect. He's ~~a great combo of~~ funny and strict. He

dances with the vacuum cleaner, and he makes the kids do their

homework. After a while, they figure out who he is. They don't

tell their mom, though. They love having him around!

The funniest scene is in a restaurant. He has to have dinner

as himself and at another table as the nanny. He runs to the

Add a sentence to make a description more complete.

rest room to switch back and forth. Another time, he orders
He finds sneaky ways to make his ex-wife's boyfriend look bad.
fancy take-out food and pretends he cooked it.

Revise a sentence to add important detail.

in a goofy kind of way
Mrs. Doubtfire was a huge hit. It is funny. I recommend this
who likes to laugh—kids or grown-ups
movie to anybody!

Change the recommendation to be more precise.

Go ahead now and revise your writing. Read your draft carefully. As you find things you want to change, mark your draft with these changes. Reread your review as you make changes to be sure that it still makes sense. Keep revising until you really like what you've written. Use the Revising Checklist as a guide to help you revise.

Revising Marks

≡ capitalize
∧ add
✐ remove
⊙ add a period
／ make lowercase
◯ move
↻ transpose

Revising Checklist

- Does the review give a clear idea of what the movie is like?
- Are the key events and characters described?
- Does the review offer an opinion and explain it in a convincing way?
- Is the writing clear and easy to understand?
- Can you add humor or examples to tell the reader more about the movie?
- Is the tone of your review appropriate for the movie?
- Do you have enough reasons and details to support your opinion?

Writer's Tip
Not every problem requires major rewriting. Sometimes a tiny change in wording or punctuation is all that is needed.

Portfolio
Remember to clip all your drafts together. Don't let any get lost.

Conferencing

Read your review to a classmate. Then, ask your partner to go over the questions in the Revising Checklist with you. Talk about the ideas your partner has to make your review better.

Become a Super Writer

Mood is important in stories. It can make your writing more effective. To learn more about mood, see page 228 in the *Writer's Handbook* section.

Polish Your Writing

Lloyd revised his movie review several times. With this draft, he thought he had finally said what he wanted to say. Before he published his review, he went through it again to edit and proofread it.

Underline the movie title or put it in italics.

Add a comma to a compound sentence.

Replace a noun with a pronoun.

Combine two short sentences.

Fix a run-on with a comma and the word *but*.

Correct a spelling mistake that the Spelling tool didn't catch.

Dad in a Dress!
by Lloyd Williams

<u>Mrs. Doubtfire</u> is a wacky movie starring Robin Williams. He is a man who dresses up as a lady. When he gets divorced, he hardly ever gets to see his kids. He misses them, so he dresses up as a grandmother-type and gets hired as their nanny. ~~His kids~~ They don't recognize him, because ~~He~~ He wears a wig and a dress. He also uses a funny voice. It isn't very believable, but it makes for one strange scene after another.

As a dad, he was a flake, but when he is Mrs. Doubtfire, he (or she?) is perfect. He's funny and strict. He dances with the vacuum cleaner, and he makes the kids do their homework. After a while, they figure out who he is. They don't tell their mom, though. They love having him around!

The funniest scene is in a restaurant. He has to have dinner as himself and at another table as the nanny. He runs to the (rest room) restroom to switch back and forth. Another time, he orders fancy take-out food and pretends he cooked it. He finds sneaky ways to make his ex-wife's boyfriend look bad.

<u>Mrs. Doubtfire</u> was a huge hit. It is funny in a goofy kind of way.

Your review is almost ready to share with others. Before you publish it, read it over carefully. Search for grammar, spelling, and punctuation mistakes. Correct them, using the Proofreading Marks. The Editing and Proofreading Checklist can help you. It lists some things to keep in mind as you polish your work.

Proofreading Marks

⁋	indent first line of paragraph
≡	capitalize
∧ or ∨	add
ℓ	remove
⊙	add a period
/	make lowercase
◯	spelling mistake
∼	move
∼	transpose

Editing and Proofreading Checklist

- Did I use <u>I</u> and <u>me</u> correctly?

  *See page 262 in the **Writer's Handbook** section.*

- Do my verbs agree with their subjects?

  *See page 255 in the **Writer's Handbook** section.*

- Did I use punctuation marks correctly?

  *See page 270 in the **Writer's Handbook** section.*

- Do I need to fix any sentence errors, such as run-ons or fragments?

  *See pages 245–246 in the **Writer's Handbook** section.*

- Does my title need punctuation?

  *See pages 272–273 in the **Writer's Handbook** section.*

- How's my spelling? Does it need work?

  *See page 275 in the **Writer's Handbook** section.*

Writer's Tip
When you edit, read carefully to be sure you've actually written down what you meant to write.

Portfolio
Save every draft in your portfolio until your final copy is completed.

Conferencing

Ask a classmate to read your review. Can your partner find any sentences that have mistakes? Discuss any errors that are found and take notes about the suggestions.

Become a Super Writer

Be sure you write titles correctly. For help using quotation marks, italics, or underlining with titles, see pages 272–273 in the *Writer's Handbook* section. For help in capitalizing titles, see page 266 in the *Writer's Handbook* section.

Share Your Work

Lloyd was ready to share his review with an audience. He found out that one of his classmates had also written a review of *Mrs. Doubtfire,* so together they decided to discuss their reviews in front of the class.

Dad in a Dress!
by Lloyd Williams

Mrs. Doubtfire is a wacky movie starring Robin Williams. He is a man who dresses up as a lady. When he gets divorced, he hardly ever gets to see his kids. He misses them, so he dresses up as a grandmother-type and gets hired as their nanny. They don't recognize him because he wears a wig and a dress. He also uses a funny voice. It isn't very believable, but it makes for one strange scene after another.

As a dad, he was a flake, but when he is Mrs. Doubtfire, he (or she?) is perfect. He's funny and strict. He dances with the vacuum cleaner, and he makes the kids do their homework. After a while, they figure out who he is. They don't tell their mom, though. They love having him around!

The funniest scene is in a restaurant. He has to have dinner as himself and at another table as the nanny. He runs to the restroom to switch back and forth. Another time, he orders fancy take-out food and pretends he cooked it. He finds sneaky ways to make his ex-wife's boyfriend look bad.

Mrs. Doubtfire was a huge hit. It is funny in a goofy kind of way. I recommend this movie to anybody who likes to laugh—kids or grown-ups!

Does your review do a convincing job? Do you think others might follow your recommendation? Share your review with an audience to find out! Choose a way to publish it.

Two Thumbs . . . Up or Down? ▶

Did anyone in your class review the same movie that you reviewed? In front of a group, discuss the movie together. Offer your main points, and then talk about what you agreed on and what struck each of you differently. Keep it friendly!

◀Put It in Print

Would once-a-month reviews help you choose books, movies, and CDs? Make a magazine of reviews written by the class. Give your magazine a catchy title. Create sections for reviews of movies, books, and music. Make copies for everyone to take home. Then, do it all again next month!

Talk It Up ▶

If your classroom is set up to do video conferencing, contact a fifth-grade class in another state and share your class's movie reviews. Afterward, invite the other class to ask your classmates questions. If the other class is familiar with the movies, ask them to give their opinions, too.

Writing a Speech

Great **speeches** have the power to move nations. Sometimes it is the words that stir the audience. Other times it is the fire in the speaker's voice.

Martin Luther King, Jr., gave his famous "I Have a Dream" speech at a civil rights rally in Washington, D.C., in 1963. The words he spoke that day have lived in the hearts and minds of millions of people ever since. Part of that speech is shown here and on page 201.

> **The speaker introduces his main idea.**

> **The speaker uses a quotation at the beginning to get the listeners' attention.**

> **Dramatic voice is used to convince or persuade the listener.**

"I Have a Dream"

I say to you today, my friends, that even though we face the difficulties of today and tomorrow, I still have a dream. . . . I have a dream that one day this nation will rise up and live out the true meaning of its creed— "We hold these truths to be self-evident, that all men are created equal."

I have a dream that one day on the red hills of Georgia, the sons of former slaves and the sons of former slave owners will be able to sit down together at the table of brotherhood.

I have a dream that one day even the state of Mississippi. . . . will be transformed into an oasis of freedom and justice.

I have a dream that my four little children will one day live in a nation where they will not be judged by the color of their skin but by the content of their character. . . .

Talk About the Model

As a Reader

★ What is the speaker's dream?

★ What does Dr. King want his listeners to do?

As a Writer

★ Why do you think Dr. King repeated phrases like *I have a dream?*

★ Why do you think Dr. King included words from the patriotic song "My Country, 'Tis of Thee"?

This will be the day when all of God's children will be able to sing with new meaning— "My country 'tis of thee let freedom ring"— and if America is to be a great nation, this must become true.

So let freedom ring from the prodigious hilltops of New Hampshire. Let freedom ring from the mighty mountains of New York . . . But not only that. . . . Let freedom ring from every hill and molehill of Mississippi. . . .

. . . . When we let freedom ring from every village and every hamlet, from every state and every city, we will be able to speed up that day when all of God's children— black men and white men, Jews and Gentiles, Protestants and Catholics—will be able to join hands and sing in the words of that old Negro spiritual, "Free at last, free at last, thank God Almighty, we are free at last."

The speaker gives an example of what he hopes will happen.

The speaker uses an example to add information.

Examples make the ideas apply to many people and places.

The speaker repeats a phrase for emphasis.

The speech ends with a summary and a call to action.

Make a Plan

Create a plan to help you write your speech.

Choose Your Topic

Start by choosing a topic.

- Select a topic you know a lot about. It should be one that you and your listeners are interested in. It could be your solution to some local or national problem, or it could be your ideas about how something should be done.

- Write down everything you know about your topic.

Learn More About Your Topic

Next, find more information about your topic.

- Take careful notes.

- Look for interesting stories, facts, or quotations. These can be used to grab your listeners' attention at the start of your speech and to give important details in the body of your speech.

Organize Your Speech

Once you've researched your topic, organize your speech with an outline that has an introduction, a body, and a conclusion. Use the model on the left as a guide.

Title

I.   Introduction

A. Main idea or opinion

B. Quotation, fact, or story to support main idea

II. Body

A. Most important idea

1. Facts and examples

2. Facts and examples

B. Next most important idea

1. Facts and examples

2. Facts and examples

III. Conclusion

A. Main idea restated

B. Summary of why topic is important

Write It Down

As you write your speech, follow your outline and keep your purpose and audience in mind.

Introduce Your Topic

- Present an interesting story, fact, or quotation to get your listeners' attention.
- State the main idea of your speech.

Develop the Body of the Speech

- Give your opinion clearly and forcefully.
- Tell your main ideas in order of importance.
- Add facts and examples to support your opinion.
- Use dramatic voice to convince or persuade your readers about your topic.

Bring Your Speech to a Close

- Conclude your speech by stating the main idea again at the end.
- Repeat for your listeners why you believe your topic is so important. Ask them to act on it in some way.

Conferencing

Read your speech to a partner. Ask how convincing your speech is. Where do you need stronger reasons or examples?

Look It Over

Reread your speech. Do your ideas flow smoothly? Did you use dramatic voice? Are your grammar and spelling correct? Do your pronouns agree with their antecedents? Remember that you can always go back and revise your writing. If you decide to publish your speech, be sure to edit and proofread it.

EQUAL RIGHTS NOW!

Tech Tip

If you read your speech to an audience, print it in large, bold type so the words will be easy to see.

Portfolio

If you plan to polish your speech further, keep it in the Works in Progress section.

FIRST-CLASS CITIZENSHIP NOW

Give Your Speech

If you decide to share your speech, use these tips and guidelines to help you get ready to deliver it.

Use Notes or Your Final Copy

When you give your speech, you can read aloud your final copy. Your speech may sound better and people may pay more attention if you speak from notes instead. To do this, follow these tips.

- Write the important ideas on index cards.
- Arrange the cards in the correct order for your speech.
- Then, practice, practice, practice until you can deliver your speech smoothly and easily.

Speaking Guidelines

- Stand tall but relaxed.
- Rehearse your speech several times in front of a mirror, and then for friends or family members.
- Take your time as you speak.
- Hold your head up and speak in a strong voice. If you use notes, hold them at an easy-to-read distance that doesn't block your face.
- Make eye contact with your audience between sentences. If this is uncomfortable, look just above your audiences heads.
- If your hands are shaky, hold on to the edge of a desk.

As I See It!

Have you ever seen an argument turn into shouts of "Yes, it is!" and "No, it isn't!"? Two people often see the same thing in different ways. Is it a ball or a strike? Was the roller-coaster ride good or was it terrible?

When you write a **point-of-view essay,** you give your viewpoint about a topic you feel strongly about. You back up your ideas with facts and do your best to convince readers to agree that you're right.

Meet the Writer

Divorce hits kids hard, and I wanted to tell the world my opinion about the topic.

Lisa Crooks
Iowa

A Point-of-View Essay

★ Has a topic that is meaningful to the writer
★ Gives facts and details that support the writer's opinion
★ Tries to convince others to share the writer's viewpoint
★ Is well organized, with a definite introduction, body, and conclusion

Prewriting

Think It Through

To start your point-of-view essay, you need to select a topic that you know and feel strongly about.

Brainstorming

Sit quietly and think about possible topics to write about. Lots of ideas will probably occur to you, but check your journal and log for more.

Now it's your turn to list topic ideas. Think of topics that get your feelings flowing. Jot down a list of possible topics on a sheet of paper. Circle the topics on your list that you have the strongest opinions about.

Lisa's List

- tattletales
- people who don't write back
- divorce
- snobby kids who brag
- violent movies

Select a Topic

Lisa chose the topic of divorce from her list of ideas. Choose the topic that you want to develop for your point-of-view essay.

- Which topic do you keep coming back to?
- Which topic do you know the most about?
- Tell yourself in one sentence what your point of view about the topic is.

Will There Be Soccer in Kimball School?

Does Divorce Affect Kids?

Design a Plan

Lisa made a plan for her essay. She wrote the headings *Introduction, Body,* and *Conclusion* at the top of three separate note cards. As she thought about her topic, she wrote down ideas and details where she thought they belonged.

The writer identifies the topic and gives her viewpoint.

The writer gives facts and details to back up her ideas.

The writer sums up the main points and asks the reader to agree.

Introduction
Divorce is wrong when people have kids.

Divorce makes kids think it's their fault.

Body
People shouldn't marry if they are going to get divorced.

Kids feel unloved.

Conclusion
Divorce is wrong because kids need two parents.

People should marry people they want to stay married to.

Now, create your plan. Work with the topic you chose.

- Think about what you want to include in the introduction, body, and conclusion.
- Collect information that will back up your viewpoint with facts.
- Use note cards, as Lisa did, to organize your facts and ideas.

Conferencing

Ask a partner to review your plan. Are the ideas arranged in a logical order? Does your partner have any suggestions to improve your plan?

Portfolio

Store your plan. Refer to it when you write your first draft.

Drafting Put It Into Words

Once Lisa got started on her essay, she found it easy to write. To stay on track, she kept checking her note cards to see what to do next. Here is Lisa's first draft. How well did Lisa follow her plan?

Divorce Troubles
by Lisa Crooks

Tell me, why do people get married if they are just going to get divorced. A person who has a kid or has kids and gets divorced makes the kids think its their fault, even though it is not their fault.

People should not get marry if they are just going to get divorced they will hurt the kids. Doesn't it say that they will stay together in sickness and in health till death do they part? They say they do, and then they get divorced. It doesn't make any sense.

If people have kids and get divorced it could make the kids feel like they are not loved. Kids kind of know it is not their fault, but they can't help feeling it and thinking that it is their fault.

If you are reading this, please listen to me for your sake and your kids sake. I might be young. I kind of know how it feels to live with only one parent. Kids need to have both a mother and a father, so please don't get married if you don't love, care for, and plan to stay with this special person for the rest of your long life.

The writer introduces the topic and states her viewpoint.

She presents details to support her point of view.

The writer uses a pleading tone in her essay.

The writer sums up the main points and asks readers to agree.

Think Like a Writer

As you write your first draft, ask yourself

★ **Subject:** What is my topic, and what is my opinion about it?

★ **Audience:** Whom am I writing this for? Will my audience be sympathetic to my ideas?

★ **Purpose:** Why am I writing this?

★ **Form:** What are the characteristics of a point-of-view essay? How can I make sure I include them?

Now you can begin writing the first draft of your point-of-view essay. Review your notes and follow your plan. Remember who your audience is and the facts and details that you can use to help bring your audience around to your point of view. Use the following Drafting Checklist as a guide.

Drafting Checklist

- The first paragraph identifies the topic and my point of view.
- The body of the essay contains facts and details that back up my statements.
- The tone of the essay is clear and convincing.
- The conclusion summarizes my main points.
- Readers are asked to share my point of view about the topic.

Writer's Tip
Label the introduction, body, and conclusion as you write. This will help make sure things are in the right part of your essay.

Tech Tip
View the names of your files in list format. The list shows the date you last worked on a file.

Portfolio
Keep your draft in your portfolio until you are ready to revise it.

Conferencing

Read your first draft to a partner. Ask if you have included enough facts to support your opinion. Does your partner have any suggestions that might improve your essay? Consider which ideas you might want to add.

Lisa read through her essay. She paid close attention to how she expressed her ideas. She also thought about the facts and reasons she gave. She decided to make some changes. How do you think they improved her essay?

Divorce Troubles
by Lisa Crooks

Tell me, why do people get married if they are just going to get

When people have kids and get

divorced. ~~A person who has a kid or has kids and gets~~ divorced

∧

~~makes~~ the kids think its their fault, even though it is not their fault.

Rewrite a sentence to make it clearer.

People should not get marry if they are just going to get

divorced they will hurt the kids. Doesn't it say that they will stay

each say, "I do,"

together in sickness and in health till death do they part? They ~~say~~

∧

~~they do~~, and then they get divorced. It doesn't make any sense.

Add a quotation to make a sentence more interesting.

If people have kids and get divorced it could make the kids feel

,and the kids may run away

like they are not loved. Kids kind of know it is not their fault, but

∧

they can't help feeling it and thinking that it is their fault.

Add an example to support the writer's opinion.

If you are reading this, please listen to me for your sake and your

only eleven years old   , but

kids sake. I might be ~~young.~~ I kind of know how it feels to live with

∧   ∧

only one parent. Kids need to have both a mother and a father~~, so~~

Add a detail to make the writing more personal.

Combine two sentences to connect related ideas.

please don't get married if you don't love, care for, and plan to stay
═

with this special person for the rest of your long life.

Make a new, separate sentence for the ending.

Now it's time to revise your first draft. Read your essay and decide what you like about it and what you can change to make it better. You may decide to revise your essay several times. Reread it after each revision to be sure it still says what you want it to say. Use the Revising Checklist as a guide to help you make changes.

Revising Marks

≡   capitalize

∧   add

✎   remove

⊙   add a period

／   make lowercase

◠   move

∼   transpose

Revising Checklist

- Does the point-of-view essay have an appropriate tone?
- Is the essay written from my viewpoint?
- Does the essay have three parts—an introduction, a body, and a conclusion?
- Is the language appropriate for the purpose and audience?
- Are details included to make the writing interesting and personal?

Tech Tip

Be sure you don't leave in extra words when you make changes. Reread every correction you make.

Conferencing

Read your point-of-view essay to your partner, and then review the questions on the Revising Checklist with him or her. If the answer to any question is "no," talk about how you can revise your writing to improve it.

Portfolio

Keep your drafts and notes together. Clip them as soon as you finish working.

Become a Super Writer

Be sure to use facts and details to support your ideas. For help, see page 223 in the *Writer's Handbook* section.

Editing and Proofreading
Polish Your Writing

Lisa reread her last revision and thought her essay was ready for its final polishing touches. She paid attention to her grammar, capitalization, punctuation, and spelling. What corrections did she make?

Correct an end mark.

Add a comma after a clause.

Add an apostrophe to a contraction.

Correct a verb form.

Fix a run-on sentence.

Add a comma after a clause.

Use a demonstrative adjective and a noun to make the meaning clearer.

Insert an apostrophe to make a possessive noun.

Divorce Troubles
by Lisa Crooks

Tell me, why do people get married if they are just going to get

divorced. When people have kids and get divorced the kids think

it's their fault, even though it is not their fault.

married

People should not get marry if they are just going to get

, because

divorced they will hurt the kids. Doesn't it say they will stay

together in sickness and in health till death do they part? They each

say, "I do," and then they get divorced. It doesn't make any sense.

If people have kids and get divorced it could make the kids feel like

they are not loved, and the kids may run away. Kids kind of know it is

that way

not their fault, but they can't help feeling it and thinking that it

is their fault.

If you are reading this, please listen to me for your sake and your

kids sake. I might be only eleven years old, but I kind of know how it

feels to live with only one parent. Kids need to have both a mother and

a father. Please don't get married if you don't love, care for, and

plan to stay with this special person for the rest of your long life.

It's time for you to polish your point-of-view essay. Read your essay carefully and look for mistakes in grammar, spelling, capitalization, and punctuation. Use Proofreading Marks to show the changes you want to make. The Editing and Proofreading Checklist can help you.

Proofreading Marks

Mark	Meaning
¶	indent first line of paragraph
≡	capitalize
∧ or ∨	add
ℊ	remove
⊙	add a period
/	make lowercase
○	spelling mistake
⌒	move
∼	transpose

Editing and Proofreading Checklist

- Did I use contractions? Are they made correctly?
  See page 272 in the *Writer's Handbook* section.
- Did I use demonstrative adjectives to emphasize certain nouns?
  See page 257 in the *Writer's Handbook* section.
- Did I use commas, periods, question marks, and other punctuation correctly?
  See pages 269–273 in the *Writer's Handbook* section.
- Did I spell all words correctly?
  See pages 275–284 in the *Writer's Handbook* section.
- Is my handwriting neat and easy to read?
  See page 274 in the *Writer's Handbook* section.

Tech Tip
Use "Search and Replace" to delete any extra marks that might have been left when you made corrections.

Portfolio
Clip all your drafts and notes together. Put the final draft on top.

Conferencing

Have a partner read your essay. Can your partner find any errors you missed? Talk about these errors, and then make notes about how to fix them.

★ Become a Super Writer

Be sure to use common, proper, and demonstrative adjectives correctly. For help, see page 257 in the *Writer's Handbook* section.

Share Your Work

Here is Lisa's final draft. She was proud of her point-of-view essay and decided to publish it by sharing it with her classmates in a TV talk-show format.

Divorce Troubles
by Lisa Crooks

Tell me, why do people get married if they are just going to get divorced? When people have kids and get divorced, the kids think it's their fault, even though it is not their fault.

People should not get married if they are just going to get divorced, because they will hurt the kids. Doesn't it say that they will stay together in sickness and in health till death do they part? They each say, "I do," and then they get divorced. It doesn't make any sense.

If people have kids and get divorced, it could make the kids feel like they are not loved, and the kids may run away. Kids kind of know it is not their fault, but they can't help feeling that way and thinking that it is their fault.

If you are reading this, please listen to me for your sake and your kids' sake. I might be only eleven years old, but I kind of know how it feels to live with only one parent. Kids need to have both a mother and a father. Please don't get married if you don't love, care for, and plan to stay with this special person for the rest of your long life.

Here are some suggestions for publishing your point-of-view essay. Choose the one you like best or use an idea of your own.

TV Talk Show ▶

Host a TV talk show. Read your essay to your audience, and then ask for their comments. Expect your audience to have opinions that are the same as and different from yours. Allow everyone who wishes to share their own opinion and comments.

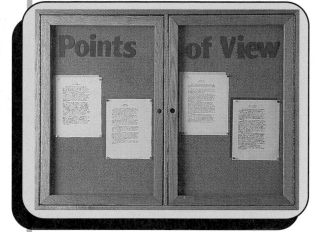

◀ Bulletin-Board Display

Work with a small group to create a bulletin-board display of your essays. Talk with your teacher about places to set up the display—your classroom, the hallway or the library, the school's main entrance, or some other location. Add a catchy title and colorful illustrations and pictures.

Op-Ed Page ▶

Many newspapers print point-of-view essays on a special page, called the opinion or op-ed page, that faces the editorial page. Print two to four essays together to create an op-ed page of your own. Use your computer to make your essays look like those on a newspaper page. Share your op-ed page with others.

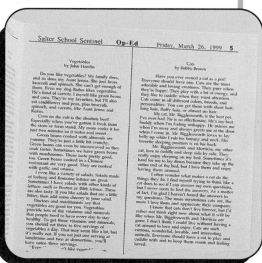

Audiotapes

Get together with other classmates and make an audiotape of your essays. Practice speaking your essays before you make your recording. Then, play the tape for classmates, friends, and family members.

Writing a Commercial

"And now a word from our sponsor." People who watch TV or listen to the radio know that these words are used to introduce a commercial. Some **commercials** are fun to watch or listen to. Others can be loud and annoying.

"Not Just Pets" was written to advertise a business run by kids. The writer uses dialogue to make his commercial realistic and convincing.

Meet the Writer

My favorite radio station lets kids put on free ads. So I wrote this commercial for the dog, cat, and plant service my friends and I run.

Andy Janovic
Pennsylvania

> The writer uses dialogue to catch the listeners' attention.

"Not Just Pets"
by Andy Janovic

Mr. Benson: Hello, Andy. Going to the game?

Andy: Hi, Mr. Benson. Not today. The Crofts are away, and I'm going over to feed their cats.

Mr. Benson: It seems every time I see you, you're either walking dogs, watering plants, or taking care of someone's cats!

Andy: Yeah, well, we have this service called "Not Just Pets."

Mr. Benson: Who's "we"?

Andy: "Not Just Pets" is a bunch of kids who take care of people's pets and plants while they're away. When people hire a "Not Just Pets" kid, they don't have to worry. We take care of their pets and plants, and we do it on time! Plus, the pets and plants love us!

The next time you go away, we can take care of Jake for you. Got to run now. "Not Just Pets" has a job to do!

> He repeats the product's name for emphasis.

> The writer gives reasons why the product is good.

> He repeats the name again so listeners will remember it.

Talk About the Model

★ Do you think this commercial will create business for "Not Just Pets"?

★ What are the best reasons the writer gives?

★ How does the writer make the dialogue sound realistic?

★ How does the writer get you to remember the product and its name?

Make a Plan

Writing commercials is fun. To get started, you need a plan.

Choose a Product or Service

Think of a product or service you could sell. Maybe you make jewelry, bake cookies, or rake leaves. Perhaps your science-fair invention or computer game would be a big hit. Brainstorm a list of things you could sell, and then choose one to advertise in your commercial.

Tell How Your Product or Service Is Useful

When you've picked a product or service, use a chart like the one on the left to get information for a 30- to 60-second commercial.

Product or service:

Product's name:

Product's description:

1.

2.

3.

Reasons why people would want it:

1.

2.

3.

Organize Your Writing

Organize your commercial with an introduction, a body, and a conclusion. Introduce your product or service in the introduction. In the body, tell more about the product and why people will want to use it. Wrap up your commercial in the conclusion.

Write It Down

Consider writing your commercial as a dialogue between two characters. Have one character "sell" the other character the product or service.

Start Off Right

Catch your listeners' attention with a strong beginning. Introduce your product or service with dialogue or with an interesting statement, quotation, or question.

Provide Important Details

- Give two or three convincing reasons why someone would want your product or service.

- Use vivid, sensory words to describe the product. Pretend that your listeners have never seen, heard, smelled, touched, or felt this product before. Help them to know what it's like.

- Use slang or dialect if it would help you sell your product to a specific audience that understands the slang or dialect. Slang, very informal language, and dialect, the language used locally by a group of people, can be effective in some commercials.

- Find two key words that you can use to describe the product and repeat them often.

Close the Sale

Bring your commercial to a close. Restate your topic and sum up why listeners would want to use your special product.

Conferencing

Read your commercial to a partner. Would your partner want to buy your product or service? Are the name and description easy to remember?

Look It Over

Did you use dialogue effectively in your commercial? Does the introduction get listeners interested in your product or service? If you plan to publish your commercial, remember to revise, edit, and proofread your writing.

Tech Tip

Ask your teacher how to automatically indent lines after the first one when you type dialogue.

Portfolio

Store your commercial until you are ready to act it out or videotape it.

Not Just Pets
Pet Sitting and Plant Watering Service

789 Barren Ave.
Bethlehem, PA 18015

Andy Janovic
(999) 123-4567

WRITER'S HANDBOOK

WRITER'S CRAFT

Alliteration means repeating the same beginning consonant sound in a group of words. Alliteration creates interesting sound effects for readers. It can add humor to writing and makes words fun to read.

> Munching a muffin, the girl said, "More milk, please."
>
> Sammy sipped soup and ate spinach salad.
>
> Two tigers twisted their tails together as they played on the plain.
>
> Floating feathers flip and fly as they fall from the sky.

Spice up the stories and poems you're writing by using alliteration.

An **analogy** compares something new to something familiar and points to similarities between them.

> The grand opening of the new store looked just like a birthday party. Balloons decorated the walls. Streamers hung from the lights. Laughter and lively music filled our ears. The store felt like a fun place to shop.

When you use an analogy, you use something familiar, like a birthday party, to make the scene clear to your readers. The more points of similarity you show, the stronger you make the comparison.

Analogies work especially well when you write to describe, to inform, or to persuade.

> **Remember:**
> Use an analogy when you want a creative way to make a comparison.

Character

A **character** is a person in a story. Sometimes the character is an animal that acts like a person.

Stories usually have two or more characters. The main character is the one who is faced with a problem or conflict. The other characters either help the main character, make trouble for the main character, or help the story's events to move along.

When you write, try to create interesting characters who are like real people, growing and changing as the story develops.

Characterization

Writers try to make characters "come alive" for readers. This is called **characterization**. To do this, writers introduce and develop their story's characters so that the characters seem real to the reader.

Remember:
Make your characters seem real by showing what they think and feel.

Writers can describe a character's appearance, personality, accomplishments, and other details, using vivid, sensory words and phrases. Writers can show what the character thinks and feels, and show how the character interacts with other characters in the story. Dialogue can also be used to let the character speak for himself or herself. Readers can learn a lot about a character through the character's conversations.

Rhoda, our mail carrier, always has a big smile on her face. Yesterday, though, with the saddest look on her face, she told me that her parrot, Walter, was missing.

"Maybe a bunch of us could look for Walter," I said.

"It won't do much good," she said hopelessly. "He's probably lost forever."

Details create a picture for the reader. They help readers see and understand what the writer is trying to say.

Sensory words describe what people see, hear, smell, taste, and feel.

> I love to eat fresh fish when it's baked or broiled. Just to smell fish cooking makes me hungry. The skin is crisp and crunchy. At just the touch of a fork, the fish flakes into small, tasty morsels.

Try to include as many senses as you can so that your readers will experience what you are describing.

Remember:
A *sweet, juicy, jumbo strawberry* creates a tempting picture.

Examples are facts that support a writer's opinions.

Opinion: Skateboarders need a place of their own.

Examples: Store owners complain about the noise that skateboards make.

Bike riders get angry when skateboarders clog the bike lanes.

Ramps could be built in a part of Graham Park where walkers wouldn't be disturbed.

Examples are especially important to include when you are writing to inform or persuade.

Dialogue and Quotations

Dialogue is conversation between two or more people in a story. Writers use dialogue to let readers discover what characters are thinking and feeling.

"Did you see the pink buds on the rosebushes?" Lucia asked.

"I guess the plants survived the frost," Tony said.

When you write dialogue, put quotation marks at the beginning and end of the speaker's exact words.
▶ **For help with quotation marks, see page 273.**

Quotations are the exact words a person says or writes. When you interview someone, take careful notes. Better yet, use a tape recorder. Always quote a speaker or a writer word-for-word when you use a quotation in your writing.

Exaggeration

Exaggeration is using words to make a person or a thing seem larger or greater than it really is. Writers use exaggeration to make a point or to entertain their readers.

One day a bluebird the size of a passenger plane landed on our bird feeder. From inside the house, I could hear it crunching on the seeds. I'm just glad it didn't land on my head!

The flies are so large this summer. I think I'll use a lasso instead of a fly swatter. I might just catch one as they come charging in for a landing.

You should vote for me for class president. I'm the smartest, the biggest, the bravest, and the best friend you have.

When you write to amuse your audience, use exaggeration to describe your subject in a larger-than-life way. When you write to persuade, use exaggeration to make your opinion seem important.

A **flashback** interrupts a story to show what happened at an earlier time. Writers often use flashbacks to fill in information that readers need to know.

> Caroline sat next to Grandpa's hospital bed. It seemed like only yesterday that he had taken her to the amusement park. She knew she would never have gotten on that roller coaster without Grandpa. For giving her courage, she loved that man more than she could say.

When you write a story, use flashbacks to give your readers background information about characters.

Suspense is the feeling audiences experience when they wonder what will happen next and how stories or plays will end. Writers sometimes build suspense by giving hints about what may or may not happen. This technique is called **foreshadowing.**

> Strange things were happening. One day a pair of my jeans disappeared from the clothesline. Another time, a bag filled with stale bagels was left at the back door. My whole family was puzzled. Who was behind these *mysterious* happenings?

When you write a story, use foreshadowing to keep your readers eagerly reading until the very end.

Remember: Make each event build suspense and pull your reader deeper into the story.

Humor

Humor is what makes people laugh. When writers describe something humorous, they try to build up to the ending, just as if they were telling a joke.

> No matter how hard I tried, I couldn't put the ball through the hoop. I shot from far away. I shot from close up. The ball kept bouncing out. No one told me it was a trick basket with a narrow rim.

You can use humor in stories. You can also use humor when you write to persuade.

Idiom

An **idiom** is an everyday expression that means something different from its actual word-for-word meaning. Writers use idioms to make dialogue seem like real speech.

> Idiom: The news knocked my socks off.
>
> Meaning: The news came as a total surprise.

Irony

Irony is using words to say one thing but mean the opposite. A writer can use a simple kind of irony in a character's words.

> Soaked to the skin, Chris said very grumpily, "I really love rain."

Sometimes writers make irony part of the plot. For example, a writer could make a character believe that something will happen, even though readers know that it will not.

> Becky, who cannot carry a tune, convinces herself she will win the music award.

> **Remember:**
> Give your audience lots of clues to let them know you're using irony.

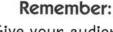

To help them choose their words carefully, writers must think about their reason for writing—the purpose. They must also consider who will read their work—the audience.

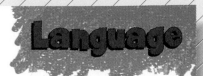

Formal and Informal

A person who writes a letter to the editor of a local newspaper should use **formal language**. That person is writing to an adult audience for a serious reason.

> Our town needs a Youth Council to help the mayor plan cultural events for young people.

In a letter to a friend, however, someone would use **informal language**. It matches the purpose of a friendly letter.

> Guess what? I'm on the Youth Council. Our first meeting is next week, and I'm really excited.

Remember: Choose the kind of language that matches your purpose.

Slang and Dialect

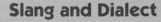

Slang is very informal language. Most writers avoid using slang unless they are writing dialogue or want to sound very hip and up-to-date.

A **dialect** is a version of a language spoken in a particular region or by a particular group of people. Writers use dialect to add a local flavor to their words.

Slang: He's from the old 'hood. ("neighborhood")

Dialect: He my homey. ("homeboy," or someone from the same place as you)

Literal and Figurative

Most words can be used in both a literal and a figurative way. The **literal** meaning of a word is its exact meaning. **Figurative language** uses words in an imaginative way.

Literal: They went to sea in a fishing boat.

Figurative: The future is a sea of possibilities.

▶ For more information on figurative language, see **metaphor and simile, on pages 228 and 238.**

Metaphor

A **metaphor** is a comparison that suggests how two different things are alike in some way.

> Grandma's laughter is music to my ears.
>
> For me, math is a climb up Mount Everest.

Writers use metaphors to create a feeling or to help readers picture whatever is being described. Metaphors work especially well in creative writing, such as poetry, stories, and personal narratives.

Metaphors are different from similes, which use *like* or *as* to make direct comparisons.

▶ **For help with similes, see page 238.**

Mood and Tone

Mood is the feeling that a writer creates about a place, person, or event. The setting, dialogue, and language help writers achieve the mood they want.

> With a mug of cocoa in my hand and wood crackling in the fireplace, I stood at the window, watching the snowflakes fall.

> As the sky darkened and the afternoon breezes turned into snarling winds, I huddled fearfully under the covers. Cautiously, I watched as the tree branches beat the driving rain, twisting it this way and that.

Tone is the way a writer uses words to show his or her feelings about a subject, character, or audience. The tone may be serious, sad, annoyed, or lighthearted. In the first paragraph, the writer's tone is one of annoyance and frustration. The second paragraph has a humorous tone.

> Every time I call your toll-free telephone number, I get a busy signal. It's so frustrating! Today, I ordered five kites from another company.

> For an overnight trip to the basement, I packed my radio, headphones, science-fiction stories, flashlight, pillow, and sleeping bag. I thought we might run out of supplies, so I told my friend Roger to bring magazines and extra batteries.

Onomatopoeia means using words that imitate sounds. *Thud!* for the sound that a heavy object makes when it hits the floor is an example.

Whit-wheet. Whit-wheet. "Listen! That's a curve-billed thrasher calling its mate," *Eddie said.*

You can fill a story or a poem with interesting sounds by using onomatopoeia. By listening to everyday sounds, you can collect examples for your writing.

Remember:
You can have a horse *whinny* a greeting or *clop-clop, clop-clop* when it passes in a parade.

Order of Ideas and Events

Writers want to present their ideas in a way that makes sense and keeps readers interested. There are three ways to **order ideas and events** in writing: time, space, and importance.

Time

When writing to tell a story, the best order of events is time order. **Time order** is the order in which events happen. Words like *first, next*, and *last* will help your readers follow your story.

Space

When writing to describe, writers use **space order**. They guide the reader's eyes from left to right, from front to back, or in any other pattern that makes sense. Words like *in front of* and *behind* help show where things are.

Importance

Writers use **order of importance** when writing to inform or persuade. They start with their most important idea. Then they discuss their next best ideas until they end with the least important one. They use words like *most important* and *first of all* to keep readers on track.

Organization

Many forms of writing have a clear beginning, middle, and end. Forms like speeches, point-of-view essays, and commercials are **organized** by introduction, body, and conclusion.

Beginning

The **beginning** should catch the reader's attention. Introduce the characters, setting, or problem if you are telling a story. For informative and descriptive writing, start with a topic sentence. Sometimes, starting with a question or a quotation can grab the reader's interest.

Middle

The **middle** tells the main events in a story's plot, or it gives details about a topic. Put your story events, ideas, or facts in an order that makes sense. Include only the events or details that really relate to your story or topic.

End

The **end** tells what finally happens in a story, or it sums up your main ideas. In some writing forms, it is also where you resolve a problem or draw a conclusion. A surprise ending can add interest for readers if it works for your story's plot.

Introduction

Begin with the most important idea or opinion. Add a quotation, fact, or story to support your main idea. Some speeches state all the main ideas in the **introduction**.

Body

In the **body**, write the next most important ideas or opinions, and add supporting facts and examples for each. In some speeches, the body is where all the main ideas are explored, using lots of supporting facts, examples, and quotations.

Conclusion

In the **conclusion,** restate your main idea and summarize why it's important. If you're writing a speech that presented all its main ideas in the introduction, be sure to restate all the ideas in your conclusion.

Pacing is the technique a writer uses to set or change the speed or tempo in a story. Action and dialogue will quicken the pace of a story. A lot of description and flashbacks will slow the pace. Notice below how the pace in this passage changes to match the character's mood.

> "Wow, I'll be in big trouble if I'm late for dinner again!" Daria announced. She hopped on her bike and rode off as quickly as she could.
>
> About halfway home, she stopped to drink some water. The nearby meadow was filled with wildflowers of every color. Daria remembered the wonderful picnic her family had there last spring. Daria slowly sipped some water and then got back on her bike.

The next time you write a story, use pacing to set or change the tempo.

Writers use **personification** to give human qualities to something that is not a human being.

> The dog scolded the cat next door.
>
> The buds teased us into believing that spring was near.

Personification creates pictures in a reader's mind. These pictures, along with the pictures that metaphors and similes create, help readers see, hear, or feel what happened in a new way. Use personification in stories and poems to create vivid pictures for your readers.

Personification

Remember:
Use personification to make a thing or an animal seem human.

Plot

The **plot** is what happens in a story. Writers make sure that the series of events in a plot build on one another from beginning to end.

A plot has a **beginning**, in which the stage is set for what will happen. In the **middle**, excitement builds to keep readers in suspense as the story moves toward a **high point**, or **climax**. The **end**, or **conclusion**, shows how everything turns out. Before you write, decide what the high point of your story will be. Build up to the high point and use flashback, foreshadowing, and suspense to make your characters and story events seem real.

▶ **For help with foreshadowing, suspense, and flashback, see page 225.**

Remember:
Pick one point of view and stick with it.

Point of View

In a story, the **point of view** identifies who the storyteller is. A writer chooses the point of view that will work best for the type of story he or she wishes to tell.

First Person

In the **first-person** point of view, the storyteller is one of the characters. The writer uses words such as *I* and *me* to tell what the storyteller did and saw.

> Marcy has only a few friends at school because everybody thinks she's a snob. I think she's just shy.

Third Person

In the **third-person** point of view, the storyteller is someone outside the story. The writer uses words such as *she, he*, and *they* to tell what happened.

> Out of breath, Joseph dashed into the room. "We won! We won!" he yelled. "This letter says we won a computer!"

When you write a story, use the point of view best suited to the story you are telling.

In a story, the **problem** is the obstacle or difficulty the main character must overcome. All the events in the story center on the problem and what happens because of it.

The problem can be a personal struggle inside a character.

> Ronald regrets the lie he told about Martin.

The problem can also be between two people or between a character and an outside force.

> Terri and Jo argue about who should be the softball team's captain.

> A rock slide forces a family to abandon its home.

When you write a story, choose a problem that develops naturally from the story or the characters involved.

Good writers know how to catch a **reader's interest** early on and keep the reader "hooked" until the end of the story.

Title

A good **title** grabs the reader's attention. The title should tease the reader without giving away the plot.

> For a mystery story: "Lock Without a Key"
> For a science-fiction story: "Planet Nowhere"

Beginning

A good **beginning** makes readers want to keep reading. Here is one way to begin a report about steam trains.

> Compared with today's powerful trains, steam trains are noisy and smoky and slow. However, they are also a beautiful and majestic part of our national heritage.

End

The **end** should always make a reader feel satisfied. To do that, the writer makes sure the end of a story tells what finally happened. When writing to inform or persuade, writers end by reminding people what their main ideas are.

Repetition

Repeating a word or phrase is called **repetition**. Writers use repetition in poems and other kinds of writing to add rhythm or to emphasize a certain idea.

To add rhythm:
We'll weather the weather
Whatever the weather
Whether we like it or not.

To add emphasis:
Hockey is a sport. Soccer is a sport.
Swimming is a sport. Sleeping is not.

When you write, repeat a word or phrase to add rhythm to a poem or to emphasize a certain idea.

Rhyme

When writers use **rhyme**, they repeat similar sounds at the ends of words. Many poems contain end rhymes. Because the first two and the second two lines in this poem rhyme, each pair of lines is called a rhyming couplet.

My favorite day
Is a Sunday in May.

The butterflies are in colorful flight.
And the day is longer than the night.

Verse that rhymes is pleasing to a reader's ear. Your poem can be silly or serious, depending on the rhymes you pick.

Remember:
You can find a dictionary of rhyming words in the library.

Writers sometimes repeat sounds within or at the beginnings or ends of words to create interesting sound effects. Writers use assonance and consonance to add smoothness to poems and paragraphs.

To create **assonance,** repeat the vowel sound in neighboring words within a sentence.

Steer clear of deer.   "Stay and play," said Fay.

To create **consonance,** repeat the consonant sounds at the beginnings or ends of words near one another.

The slippery slope claimed another surprised collie.

Flip me a chip for my dip.

Rhythm

Rhythm is the pattern that sounds make. In many poems the rhythm follows a regular pattern. Stressed words or syllables come at certain fixed times. In this familiar verse, it's easy to tell which sounds are stressed.

Row, row, row your boat gently down the stream.

Merrily, merrily, merrily, merrily, life is but a dream.

When you write poetry, look for a natural rhythm that will create a musical pattern.

Remember:
Read your poem aloud to hear the sounds and the beat.

Sentences

Good **sentences** can make your writing clear, interesting, and easy to understand.

Variety

Writers can add appeal to their writing by using a **variety** of imperative, interrogative, exclamatory, and declarative sentences.

Marisa thought she heard a creaking sound come from somewhere down in the basement. Was she imagining it? When she heard it again, she turned to Tom. "Did you hear that?" she whispered.

Length

Writers can also capture the reader's attention by mixing in sentences of different **lengths.** This adds interest because the sentences don't all sound the same.

I made a new friend today at school. Her name is Whitney, and she's from Indiana. She bumped into me in the hallway, and all her books came spilling out of her bookbag.

Beginnings

Another way to keep the reader interested is to start your sentences in different ways. Move a word or phrase to change the **beginning** of a sentence.

Before: The city's new science museum is located at Tenth and Orchard.

After: Tenth and Orchard is the location of the city's new science museum.

The location of the city's new science museum is Tenth and Orchard.

Short, choppy sentences that contain one idea or thought each are often dull to read. By **combining sentences**, the writer can turn a string of short sentences into one smooth sentence.

Before: I have a vegetable garden. I grow tomatoes and lettuce. I also grow cucumbers and radishes.

After: I have a vegetable garden in which I grow tomatoes, lettuce, cucumbers, and radishes.

Expanding Sentences

Expanding sentences can also make writing more interesting. Writers do this by adding information.

I have a vegetable garden in which I grow beefsteak tomatoes, Bibb lettuce, cucumbers, and the largest radishes you've ever seen.

Remember:

Combining and expanding sentences can make your writing more interesting.

Expanding

Transitions

Transitions are words and phrases that link sentences. Writers use them to present their ideas smoothly and logically.

Words: First, I went to the store. Then, I met my friend.

A phrase: I help my neighbor in her garden. As her helper, I've learned a lot about gardening.

Other useful transition words and phrases are *when, before, after, until, in front of, in back of, for example,* and *in addition.*

Setting

In a story, the **setting** is the time and place in which the story's events happen. Writers often identify the setting at the very beginning of the story.

Events can take place in the past, the present, or the future. In the first sentence below, *last year* identifies the time as the past. The place is *in that big snowstorm*. The second and third sentences below tell about events that take place in the present and the future in different locations.

> We were trapped in our car in that big snowstorm last year.

> Today, we begin our vacation in the Grand Canyon.

> He sat by the lake reading a newspaper dated 2015.

Picking a unique setting for your story is one way to build interest. You can make the setting a forest, an amusement park, a classroom, another country, an imaginary world, or any place you want. You can pick a time in the past, the present, or the future.

Simile

A **simile** is a comparison that uses the words *like* or *as* to show that two unlike things are similar in some way. Writers use similes in poems and stories to help readers see something familiar in a new way.

> Her heart beat like a loud kettle drum.

> The news startled them like a clap of thunder.

> He felt as faraway as a distant star.

Some similes are overused. New ones create better images.

Overused: I am as busy as a bee.

New: I am as busy as a traffic cop in a crowded intersection.

Use similes to make comparisons when you write. **Metaphors** can also be used to make comparisons.
▶ **For help with metaphors, see page 228.**

Voice is the way writers express ideas. It depends on what and why the writer is writing. For example, a writer will use one voice to express the benefits of exercise and another to describe a day at the beach.

Lyric

Writers often write with a **lyric voice** when they write to describe. Writers also use a lyric voice when they write poetry.

I walk alone, alone in my thoughts.

These quiet times are gifts, I know.

For this is how I live and grow.

Your lyric voice lets you focus on thoughts and feelings. You pay special attention to words that paint pictures. You look for lively similes and metaphors. You try to capture a special mood and tone.

Remember:
Be sure to select a voice that suits the purpose of your writing.

Dramatic

The **dramatic voice** helps writers write dialogue in stories and in plays. They make their characters speak like real people.

When you write to persuade, you also use a dramatic voice. That voice wants to convince others that you are right about something. It speaks with respect, and it speaks with force.

Don't sit on a couch all day watching television. Get outside. Exercise. Don't sit. Do!

Narrative

The writer's **narrative voice** is a storyteller's voice. It's funny. It's serious. It builds suspense. The writer keeps readers glued to their chairs. Sometimes the writer is a character in the story. At other times, the writer tells about the characters' thoughts, feelings, and actions.

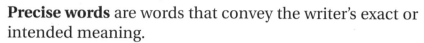

Words

Writers carefully choose the best words to make their writing clear and interesting. When writers revise their work, they double-check to see that they have chosen the right words.

Precise Words

Precise words are words that convey the writer's exact or intended meaning.

Before: Thank you for your gift. I'll use it a lot.
After: Thank you for your thoughtful and handy gift. I'll use the calculator a lot when I do my homework.

Before: We live a few blocks from the library.
After: We live on Marion Avenue, exactly two blocks east of the library.

As you check your own writing, circle any words that seem vague in meaning. These will be the words to change during the revision.

Vivid Words

Writers use **vivid words** to create colorful images in their writing. Always try to *show* your readers what you mean instead of telling them.

Before: The storm caused much damage.
After: The violent storm uprooted trees, tore roofs off houses, ripped away porches and sent cars flying.

Before: The small child yelled loudly.
After: The tiny toddler screamed so loudly that the whole world must have heard him.

A thesaurus is a helpful tool when you revise your writing.
▶ **For help in using a thesaurus, see page 286.**

> **Remember:**
> Writing is a lot like painting. Vivid words make your image come alive.

Writer's Craft

GRAMMAR, USAGE, MECHANICS, SPELLING

Sentences

A **sentence** is a group of words that expresses a complete thought. A sentence has two parts—the subject and the predicate.

Subjects

The **subject** tells who or what is doing something. It can also name who or what is being talked about.

> My friend Tanya visited the zoo.

★ Simple Subject

A **simple subject** is the main noun or pronoun in a complete subject.

> Two big white tigers slept in the sun.
>
> The golden sun glistened in the sky.

★ Complete Subject

A **complete subject** includes all the words that tell whom or what the sentence is about.

> Two big white tigers slept in the sun.
>
> The golden sun glistened in the sky.

★ Compound Subject

A **compound subject** has two or more simple subjects with the same predicate that are joined by the words *and* or *or*.

> Tanya and John will visit the zoo again.
>
> Fran or Len will go with them.

★ Understood Subject

In sentences that give commands or make requests, the subject is sometimes left out. *You* is the **understood subject** of these sentences.

> (You) Take Tyler home now.

Remember:
A sentence has a subject and a predicate, and it expresses a complete thought.

Remember:
A predicate can be just an action verb or a verb and other words that go with it.

Predicates

The **predicate** of a sentence tells what the subject does or is, or what happens to the subject.

> *Our school's basketball team* played last night.
>
> *The team* is the best in its league.
>
> *The team* has been beaten only once.

★ Simple Predicate

The **simple predicate** is the verb in the complete predicate.

> *Our team* won *last night's game.*
>
> *It* has won *every game this season.*

★ Complete Predicate

The **complete predicate** includes the simple predicate and all the words that make up the predicate part of the sentence.

> *Our team* won last night's game.
>
> *It* has won every game this season.

★ Compound Predicate

A **compound predicate** includes two or more simple predicates joined together by the words *and* or *or.*

> *The team* cheered and celebrated *with a party.*
>
> *The team* will win or lose *the national championship.*

Objects

Many sentences have an object. The **object** is the part of the sentence that receives the action. Some sentences have an indirect object as well as a direct object.

★ **Direct Object**
The **direct object** is the word that receives the action of the verb in the sentence.

> Anita painted a lovely picture.

★ **Indirect Object**
The **indirect object** tells to whom or for whom the action was done. Verbs like *give, show, buy,* and *bring* often have indirect objects.

> Anita showed Tom the picture.

Sentence Structure

Every sentence has a subject and a predicate. They can be written in different ways.

★ **Simple Sentences**
A **simple sentence** expresses one complete thought. It may have more than one subject and more than one predicate.

> Miguel enjoys gymnastics.

> His heart and lungs are growing stronger.

> Miguel exercises each day and eats healthful foods.

★ **Compound Sentences**
A **compound sentence** has two or more simple sentences that are joined by a comma and a conjunction such as *and, but, or, nor, for,* or *so.*

> Amy went to the movies, and she saw a great film.

★ **Complex Sentences**
A **complex sentence** includes a simple sentence and one or more clauses that cannot stand alone.

Simple Sentence	Clause
Amy was really happy	**because the book was exciting.**

A **phrase** is a group of words that has meaning but does not express a complete thought. Phrases can be used as adjectives, verbs, or adverbs to help make complete sentences.

adjective phrase:	in a healthful diet
verb phrase:	should begin
adverb phrase:	in early childhood
sentence:	Interest in a healthful diet should begin in early childhood.

A **clause** is a group of words that has a subject and a predicate. A clause that can stand alone is an **independent clause.** A clause that can't stand alone is called a **dependent clause.** It may begin with words like *which, who,* or *that.*

independent clause:	Alice plays badminton.
dependent clause:	which her cousins also like to play

A **fragment** is an incomplete thought. Most fragments are missing either a subject or a predicate. Correct them by adding a subject or a predicate.

fragment:	cause a lot of damage
sentence:	Natural disasters cause a lot of damage.
fragment:	the rising river
sentence:	The rising river overflowed its banks.

Remember:
A fragment is an incomplete thought. It cannot stand alone.

Run-on Sentences

A **run-on sentence** is two or more complete sentences joined without either punctuation or a conjunction. To correct a run-on, add punctuation and capitalize the next word or add a comma and a conjunction.

run-on:	Mia saw a bear she ran for help.
sentence:	Mia saw a bear. She ran for help.
sentence:	Mia saw a bear, and she ran for help.

Comma Splices

A **comma splice** has two sentences joined by a comma but with no conjunction. Add a conjunction after the comma to correct a comma splice.

incorrect:	The large black bear saw Mia, it did not chase her.
correct:	The large black bear saw Mia, but it did not chase her.

Combining and Expanding Sentences

Combining or **expanding sentences** can often improve your writing.

before:	Whales are mammals. They breathe air.
combined:	Whales are mammals and breathe air.

before:	Whales once were hunted.
expanded:	Whales once were hunted in great numbers for their meat and oil.

Remember:
You can expand sentences by adding interesting details to them.

There are four types of sentences. Each one has a specific purpose.

⭐ **Declarative Sentences**

A **declarative sentence** makes a statement or gives an opinion. A period (.) ends a declarative sentence.

> Wolves are endangered and need protection.

> I think it is important to care for wildlife.

⭐ **Interrogative Sentences**

An **interrogative sentence** asks a question. A question mark (?) ends an interrogative sentence.

> Have you ever seen a wolf?

> Do you think wolves are interesting animals?

⭐ **Exclamatory Sentences**

An **exclamatory sentence** shows strong feeling or surprise. An exclamation point (!) ends an exclamatory sentence.

> I can't believe it! I saw a wolf and her pups!

> Seeing the little wolves play was the greatest!

Remember:
Use the kind of sentence you need for each situation. For example, an exclamatory sentence is used to express excitement.

⭐ **Imperative Sentences**

An **imperative sentence** makes a request or gives a command. *You* is often the understood subject. A period (.) ends an imperative sentence.

> (You) Show Pia the wolves.

> (You) Be careful not to frighten them.

Nouns

A **noun** is a word that names a person, place, thing, or idea. A noun can be common or proper, or singular or plural.

person:	athlete	student	aunt
place:	mountain	city	kitchen
thing:	movie	car	game
idea:	fear	love	freedom

Common Nouns

A **common noun** is the general name for a person, place, thing, or idea. Common nouns are not capitalized.

person:	child	niece	librarian	writer
place:	beach	valley	theater	avenue
thing:	balloon	dream	computer	jacket
idea:	wisdom	truth	help	joy

Proper Nouns

A **proper noun** names a particular person, place, or thing. Proper nouns always begin with a capital letter.

person:	Michael Jordan	Jonas Salk	Sally Ride
place:	Oklahoma	Caribbean	Antarctica
thing:	Apollo 13	Internet	Olympics

Singular and Plural Nouns

A **singular noun** names one person, place, thing, or idea. A **plural noun** names more than one person, place, thing, or idea. Most nouns form the plural by adding *s*.

| singular: | parent | desert | radio | friendship |
| plural: | parents | deserts | radios | friendships |

Irregular nouns do not form their plurals by adding *s*.

★ **Nouns Ending in** ss, ch, sh, x, **or** zz
For singular nouns ending in *ss, ch, sh, x,* or *zz*, add *es*.

moss/mosses   bench/benches   bush/bushes

box/boxes   buzz/buzzes

★ **Nouns Ending in** y
For singular nouns ending in *y* following a consonant, change the *y* to *i* and add *es*. If the final *y* follows a vowel, simply add *s*.

baby/babies   key/keys

★ **Nouns Ending in** f **or** fe
For some nouns ending in *f* or *fe*, change the *f* to *v* and add *es*. For some nouns ending in *f* or *ff*, simply add *s*.

shelf/shelves   wife/wives
chief/chiefs   staff/staffs

★ **Nouns With Special Plural Forms**
A few nouns use the singular form for the plural.

deer/deer   sheep/sheep   moose/moose

A **possessive** noun shows possession, or ownership. Form a singular possessive noun by adding *'s*.

Meg went to her friend's house.

Form plural possessive nouns by adding an apostrophe to nouns that end in *s*. If the plural does not end in *s*, add *'s*.

The boys' soccer team won five games.

The men's team lost the same five games.

Remember:
Add 's to form singular possessive nouns—even when the singular noun ends in s.

Verbs

Every sentence must have a verb. The **verb** is the main word or words in the predicate of a sentence. A verb shows action or links the subject to another word in the sentence.

Action Verbs

An **action verb** tells what action the subject does or did.

Birds fly overhead every day.

One eagle soared into the sky.

Main Verbs and Helping Verbs

Sometimes the verb is more than one word. In this case, the **main verb** tells the most important action. The **helping verb** helps the main verb state an action or show time.

Eli has run on our track team for two years.

Eli can run several laps.

Eli is running right now.

He will run in the next track meet.

He might run in the state championships next year.

Remember:
Verbs show the action in a sentence.

Helping Verbs			
am	are	can	could
do	does	had	has
have	must	is	might
shall	should	will	would

A **linking verb** connects the subject of a sentence to a noun or an adjective in the predicate. Linking verbs tell what the subject is or is like.

noun: Luis's pet is a rabbit.

adjective: Pets are fun.

Remember:
Linking verbs tell what the subject is or is like.

★ **Forms of *Be***

The most common linking verbs are forms of the verb *be*. *Am, are, is, were, was,* and *been* are the ones used most often.

I am a soccer player.

Max and Kate are my friends.

We were all in the state finals.

Kate was happy to get an award.

She is very proud of it.

★ **Other Linking Verbs**

Other linking verbs tell what things are like or what they will become.

The food in the pot smells wonderful.

Unfortunately, it tastes too salty.

With practice, I will become a better cook.

More Linking Verbs			
appear	sound	seem	smell
become	taste	look	feel
remain	stand	grow	turn

Grammar and Usage

Verb Tenses

The **verb tense** tells when the action of a verb takes place. The three common tenses are present, past, and future. Changes in a verb's tense are shown by adding endings or using helping verbs.

★ Present Tense

The **present tense** of a verb tells about an action that is taking place now or one that takes place regularly.

> Maya performs in a local band.
>
> Maya is playing her favorite music today.
>
> She plays the trumpet every day.

★ Past Tense

The **past tense** of a verb tells about an action that took place in the past. Add *ed* to form the past tense of most verbs.

> Maya joined our band last night.
>
> Maya had joined the band before the big concert.

★ Future Tense

The **future tense** of a verb tells about an action that will take place. Use the helping verb *will* or *shall* before the main verb to show future tense.

> Our band will perform ten concerts this year.
>
> Our band shall perform only one benefit concert.

Change of Tense

Tense tells when the action of the verb takes place. Use the same tense for verbs in a sentence or paragraph—unless a **change of tense** is needed to make the meaning clear.

> incorrect: Ahmad skates every day.
>
> He practiced his jumps.
>
> correct: Ahmad skates every day.
>
> He practices his jumps.
>
> correct: Ahmad skated yesterday. He is skating right now, and he will practice his jumps tomorrow.

A verb has **principal parts**, or four basic forms. They are the present, present participle, past, and past participle. The principal parts are used to tell the time of an action.

The **present** is the basic form. It names an action in the present.

> He plays soccer at school.
>
> We close the doors.

The **present participle** ends with *ing* and is used with a form of *be*. It names an action that keeps happening.

> I am playing soccer at school.
>
> They are closing the doors.

The **past** ends with *ed*. It names an action in the past.

> She played soccer at school.
>
> They closed the doors.

The **past participle** ends with *ed* and is used with *have, has,* or *had*. It names an action that started in the past and was completed in the past.

> We have played soccer at school.
>
> He has played soccer at school.
>
> They have closed the doors.
>
> You had closed the doors.

▶ **For help with verb endings, see page 276.**

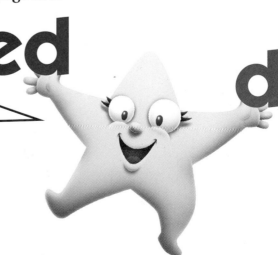

Remember:
Most verbs form their past and past participle by adding *ed* or *d* to the main verb.

Irregular Verbs

Most verbs are regular verbs. The past tense and past participle of these verbs are formed by adding *ed* to the main verb. The past and past participle of **irregular verbs** are formed in special ways.

Remember:
When you are not sure if a verb is irregular, check in the dictionary.

Irregular Verbs		
Present	Past	Past Participle
become	became	become
begin	began	begun
blow	blew	blown
catch	caught	caught
come	came	come
drink	drank	drunk
eat	ate	eaten
find	found	found
give	gave	given
go	went	gone
grow	grew	grown
know	knew	known
let	let	let
make	made	made
ride	rode	ridden
ring	rang	rung
run	ran	run
say	said	said
see	saw	seen
sing	sang	sung
sleep	slept	slept
speak	spoke	spoken
take	took	taken
tell	told	told
think	thought	thought
throw	threw	thrown
write	wrote	written

The **subject** and **verb** of a sentence must agree in number.

★ **Singular Subject**

If the subject is **singular**, make the verb singular.

> Our school band plays at all school football games.
>
> My instrument is the drum.
>
> The band leader wears a special T-shirt at the game.

Remember:

Singular means "one." Plural means "more than one."

★ **Plural Subjects**

Use a plural verb form if the subject is **plural**.

> Sometimes, other bands play at the games as well.
>
> The instruments are carried on the bus.
>
> We wear special T-shirts.

★ **Compound Subjects**

A verb also must agree with a **compound subject**. If the subjects are joined by the word *and*, the compound subject is plural.

> Amos and Lola are good musicians.
>
> Lola and her friends have a band.

Two subjects also may be joined by the word *or*. When this happens, make the verb agree with the closer subject.

> The other musicians or Lola brings the instruments on Mondays.
>
> The sax player or the trumpet players bring them on Tuesdays.

Problem Words

Some words are confusing because they are close in meaning or because some of their principal parts look alike. Be careful when using the following words.

★ Doesn't/Don't

The word **doesn't** is used with singular nouns and the pronouns *he, she,* and *it.* **Don't** is only used with *I, you, we,* and *they.*

> He doesn't water-ski anymore.

> They don't water-ski very well.

★ Rise/Raise

Rise means "to get up."
Raise means "to lift something up."

> I want to rise early.

> Raise your hands.

★ Learn/Teach

Learn means "to get information."
Teach means "to give information."

> I learn about the Internet in class.

> Afterward, I teach my whole family about it.

★ Sit/Set

Sit means "to rest" or "to remain in one place."
Set means "to put" or "to place."

> You may sit here while you wait.

> Please set the wet umbrella on the porch.

★ Lie/Lay

Lie means "to stretch oneself out in a flat position."
Lay means "to put something down."

> I would like to lie down.

> Lay the mats on the table.

★ Let/Leave

Let means "to allow."
Leave means "to go away from" or "to let stay."

> Let me help you. I will leave by six o'clock.

> I'll leave the light on for you.

An **adjective** is a word that describes a noun. Adjectives add information. They usually make what is written clearer and more interesting.

Common Adjectives

Common adjectives are words that describe people, places, things, and ideas. They tell *what kind, how many, which one,* or *how much.*

Two panthers crept through the forest.

Their sharp, alert ears suddenly pricked up.

Proper Adjectives

Some adjectives name particular persons, places, things, or ideas. Like proper nouns, **proper adjectives** begin with a capital letter.

Mr. Foxx made us New England clam chowder.

Mickey Mouse ears are easily recognized.

Remember:
Always capitalize a proper adjective.

Demonstrative Adjectives

Demonstrative adjectives are used to describe nouns. Some demonstrative adjectives describe people or things that are nearby. Others describe people or things that are far away.

use with nearby things: this, these

use with faraway things: that, those

Avoid using the words *this here, these here,* or *that there* together.

These books are the most exciting.

That book is my all-time favorite.

Those books are all special.

Adjectives

Predicate Adjectives

Adjectives usually come just before the noun they describe. **Predicate adjectives**, however, come after linking verbs like *is, seems, tastes,* or *smells* and describe the subject.

> Leah's favorite food is ready.
>
> This pasta salad tastes delicious.

Comparative Adjectives

A **comparative adjective** shows how two people, places, things, or ideas are alike or different.

To form a comparative adjective, add *er* to short adjectives. Use the word *more* with longer adjectives.

> This spaghetti is thinner than the other one.
>
> Rita's tuna salad tastes more delicious than mine.

Superlative Adjectives

A **superlative adjective** can be used to compare more than two of something. Add *est* to short adjectives, and use the word *most* with long adjectives.

> Ali is the nicest student in the class.
>
> Carlos is the most talented writer in our grade.

Remember:
Use *er* to compare two things and *est* to compare more than two of somethng.

Grammar and Usage

The words *a, an,* and *the* are special adjectives called **articles**. The article *a* is used before nouns that begin with a consonant. *An* is used before nouns that begin with a vowel. *A* and *an* are used with singular nouns. *The* can be used with singular or plural nouns.

Did you see the lizards at the zoo?

One was a bright green color with an unusual red stripe.

Remember:
Most adverbs end in *ly.*

Adverbs

An **adverb** describes a verb, an adjective, or another adverb. Adverbs can add details that tell *how* or *how much.*

describes a verb: I swiftly packed my books.

describes an adjective: I had a very important meeting.

describes an adverb: I very carefully walked outside.

Most adverbs tell *where, when, how,* or *how much* an action happens.

where?   He walked inside and closed the door.

when?   This morning, Tim left early.

how?   Hal walked slowly to the classroom.

how much?   I am extremely happy with my new bike.

Many adverbs end in *ly,* but not all do. Several common adverbs that do not end in *ly* are *seldom, always, quite, soon, then,* and *often.*

Cindy is seldom late for class.

Marla is always late for class.

I am quite prompt for class.

Comparing With Adverbs

Like adjectives, adverbs can be used to make comparisons. An adverb that compares two actions is called a **comparative adverb**. An adverb that compares more than two actions is called a **superlative adverb**.

To form comparative adverbs, add *er* to one-syllable words. Use *more* with longer adverbs and those that end with *ly*.

> Brad runs faster than his brother John.

> John runs more energetically than his brother Brad.

To form superlative adverbs, add *est* to one-syllable words. Use *most* with longer adverbs and those that end with *ly*.

> Brad runs the fastest of anyone in our grade.

> Todd runs most energetically of all.

Problem Words

The **problem words** *very* and *real* and *good* and *well* are frequently confused in writing. Use these problem words correctly as adverbs or adjectives in sentences.

★ Very/Real
Do not use *real* when you mean *very*.

| incorrect: | Gina is real nice. |
| correct: | Gina is very nice. |

★ Good/Well
Use the word *good* as an adjective and *well* as an adverb.

| incorrect: | I slept good last night. |
| correct: | I slept well last night. |

Use *well* as an adjective to describe someone's health. Use *good* with linking verbs to describe how something seems, feels, or sounds.

| correct: | The doctor said I am well. |
| correct: | Jana looks good in that red shirt. |

Negatives are words that mean "no." The adverbs *not, never, none, neither, no, seldom,* and *hardly* all are negatives. A **double negative** is the incorrect use of two negatives in the same sentence. Avoid using more than one negative in a sentence.

incorrect: I didn't get none of those grapes.

correct: I didn't get any of those grapes.

correct: I got none of those grapes.

Remember:
Use only one negative word to express one negative meaning.

Pronouns

A **pronoun** is a word that takes the place of a noun. Some pronouns replace the subject or the object of a sentence. Others are used to show ownership or to ask questions.

Lucy wants to join the soccer team.

She wants to join the soccer team.

A **subject pronoun** replaces a noun in the subject part of a sentence. Subject pronouns include *I, you, he, she, it, we, you,* and *they.*

I went to the game with a friend. We enjoyed it.

An **object pronoun** replaces a noun that follows an action verb. Object pronouns include *me, you, it, him, her, us, you,* and *them.* An object pronoun is also used after prepositions, which are words such as *to, for, in,* and *with.*

Jo went to the game with me. We enjoyed it.

Pronouns

Problem Words: *I* and *me*

I is a subject pronoun; *me* is an object pronoun. Writers sometimes misuse these words when they are part of a compound subject or object.

incorrect:	Ben and *me* went to the movies.
correct:	Ben and *I* went to the movies.
incorrect:	This is just between you and *I*.
correct:	This is just between you and *me*.

Possessive Pronouns

Possessive pronouns show ownership. Some possessive pronouns come before a noun. Others replace a noun.

I talked to Nikki about her book.

The red book is theirs.

before a noun:	my, your, his, her, its, our, their
alone:	mine, yours, his, hers, ours, theirs

Reflexive Pronouns

Reflexive pronouns refer back to the noun that is the subject of the sentence. Reflexive pronouns include *myself, yourself, himself, herself, itself, ourselves, yourselves,* and *themselves.*

Perry taught himself French.

Jimi and Ellen bought themselves new book covers.

Remember:
Reflexive pronouns only refer back to the subject of the sentence.

Remember:
Use interrogative
pronouns to ask
questions.

Interrogative Pronouns

Interrogative pronouns are used to ask questions. Common interrogative pronouns are *who, whose, which,* and *what.*

> Who will drive us to the game tomorrow?

> Which of our parents can go on the class trip?

> What places will we visit?

Pronoun Agreement

The **antecedent** of a pronoun is the noun the pronoun refers to. Pronouns always agree with their antecedents in number. Singular pronouns are used to refer to singular nouns. Plural pronouns are used to refer to plural nouns.

> singular: The team held its first game of the season.

> plural: Other teams also held their first games.

If the antecedent is compound, the pronoun should always be plural.

> Chuck and his teammates lost their game.

> Chuck's teammates and the new coach lost their game.

Pronouns should also agree with their antecedents in gender. Use *he, him,* and *his* to refer to boys and men. Use *she, her,* and *hers* to refer to girls and women. If the gender of a singular noun is unclear, use *his or her,* not *their.*

> incorrect: Every child should bring their instrument.

> correct: Every child should bring his or her instrument.

Prepositions

A **preposition** shows how a noun or pronoun is related to another word in the sentence. The words *about, around, at, before, by, down, during, from, in, of, on*, and *over* are prepositions.

Prepositional Phrases

A **prepositional phrase** is a group of words that begins with a preposition and ends with a noun or pronoun.

Our class hiked over several trails.

By the brook, we lost our way.

Object of the Preposition

The noun or pronoun that follows a preposition is called the **object of the preposition**.

We found it again near the waterfall.

Conjunctions

A **conjunction** connects individual words or groups of words. The words *and, or, but, for, so*, and *yet* are conjunctions.

The puppy and the kitten looked out the window.

The turtle or the gerbil knocked over the bowl.

Coordinating Conjunctions

A **coordinating conjunction** connects two or more words, phrases, or sentences.

We can hike in the morning and in the afternoon.

We used maps, yet we wandered from the trail.

We can meet the group at the camp, near the falls, or under the bridge.

Interjections

An **interjection** is a short exclamation that expresses strong feelings or emotions. It can express fear, anger, surprise, or happiness.

Hey! You really scared me.

Wow! What a terrific prize.

Capital letters are used to begin sentences. They are also used for proper nouns, proper adjectives, many abbreviations, and other important words in writing.

First Word of a Sentence

The first word of a sentence begins with a capital letter.

Many students in our school use computers.

Pronoun I

The **pronoun I** is always written with a capital letter.

Joe and I studied hard and passed the test.

Remember:
You are important! Always use a capital letter when you write the pronoun I.

Names and Initials

People's **names** begin with a capital letter. If a person's **initials** are used, write them in capital letters followed by periods.

Lois M. Blake   R. B. Taylor

First Word of a Direct Quotation

A **direct quotation** gives the speaker's own words. A direct quotation begins with a capital letter.

My father said, "Be sure to clean up your room."

Dialogue

Dialogue is conversation in a story or a play. Every sentence of dialogue begins with a capital letter.

"When can we leave?" asked Molly.

"At ten o'clock, I think," Tamil replied. "Everyone should be ready then."

Capitalization

Proper Nouns and Proper Adjectives

Proper nouns are the specific names of people, places, and things. A capital letter is used to begin proper nouns and the **proper adjectives** that come from these nouns.

proper noun:	My family vacationed in Hawaii.
proper adjective:	We enjoyed our week-long Hawaiian adventure.

Titles of People

A person's **official title** or **title of respect** begins with a capital. When the title is used without a name, the title is not capitalized.

Our town is led by Mayor Mary Bruno.

Is Ms. Lopez the assistant principal?

Titles of Works and Headlines

A capital letter is used to begin the first, last, and all other important words in the **title** of a book, movie, TV show, play, story, poem, or song. The **headline** of a newspaper or magazine article is often capitalized in the same way.

play:	Jo went to see *The Diary of Anne Frank*.
book:	I want to read *The Wizard of Oz*.
song:	Do you like the song "Sore Loser"?
headline:	Redwings Win Stanley Cup!

Place Names and Geographical Features

Place names are proper nouns. The name of a specific place or **geographical feature** begins with a capital letter.

We had a great time at Disney World.

The Grand Canyon is a remarkable place.

Remember:
The city, state, and country where you live begin with capital letters.

The name of a **language** or **nationality** begins with a capital.

Many Canadians speak French.

The name of a **historic event** begins with a capital.

The American Revolution began in 1773.

The first word in the **greeting** and the **closing** of a letter begins with a capital. In **addresses**, the names of streets, cities, and states begin with a capital letter.

greeting: Dear Luz,

closing: Sincerely yours,

address: 262 East Meadowlawn Drive
Midland, Texas 75050

Remember:
The names of special days begin with capital letters.

A capital letter begins the names of the **days** of the week, **months** of the year, **holidays,** and **special occasions.**

Wednesday, May 25, was Memorial Day.

Outlines are often used to plan and organize reports. Roman numerals are used before main topics in an outline. Capital letters are used before the subtopics. The **first word of the main topics** and **subtopics** begins with a capital letter.

main topic: I. Reasons for building a new gym

subtopic: A. More students in the school

subtopic: B. Old gym not air-conditioned

Citation

A **citation** gives the title, the author, and the publication data for a source of information used in a report.

The last page of your report is the bibliography. On this page, you give a list of all the sources you used in your research. The list is organized alphabetically by authors' last names, then first names. The information that follows next is the book's title, the place where the book was published, the publisher's name, and the date the book was published.

To cite information from a magazine article, you need to include the name of the magazine, the title and author of the article you used for research, the magazine issue's publication date, and the page numbers of the article.

Titles of books and magazines are set in italics if computer-printed or underlined if hand-printed. Titles of articles are set with quotation marks.

Here is one format to follow in setting up a bibliography. Notice how the items are alphabetized, indented, capitalized, and punctuated.

a book: Borillo, Carla. <u>Gila Monsters</u>. Tucson, AZ: Desert Press, 1999.

an article: Henderson, Matthew. "Javelinas, Mountain Pigs." <u>Southwest Nature</u>. Fall 1998: 68–81.

Mason, Andrea. "Finding the Questions for Your Answers." <u>Mathematics</u>. March 1998: 32–36.

Remember:
Always keep citations for all the sources you use in your research.

An **abbreviation** is a shortened form of a title or some other word or phrase. Most abbreviations begin with a capital letter. A period is used after shortened words. The two letters in states' postal abbreviations are both capitalized, but no period is used.

Dr. Poe served in the U.S. Navy.

Mrs. Towns will see you at 9:00 a.m. sharp.

Los Angeles, CA

Punctuation

Punctuation marks tell readers when to stop or pause, because something is special about the words they are reading. Punctuation marks also signal different kinds of sentences.

Indention

The first line of a paragraph is **indented**. The first word begins three spaces to the right of the left margin.

I enjoy sports because they keep me healthy. Sports can also help train your mind.

Period

Periods have many uses. Here are some of them.

★ **To End Sentences**
A statement is a sentence that tells something. Use a period at the **end of a statement.**

Bart has the lead part in the school play.

A command is a sentence that tells someone to do something. Use a period at the **end of a command.**

Meet Bart at school after play practice.

★ **In Outline Form**
Use periods **after the Roman numerals** and **capital letters** in outline parts.

main topic: I. Computers are useful and efficient

subtopic: A. Make writing tasks easier

               B. Have special features

Punctuation

Question Mark

A **question mark** is used at the end of a sentence that asks a direct question.

Has Fumiko ever been to New Hampshire?

Exclamation Point

An **exclamation point** is used at the end of a sentence or phrase that shows strong feeling or excitement.

What an exciting ride that was!

Happy New Year!

Comma

A **comma** is used to keep words, phrases, and sentence parts from running together. Commas show readers when to pause.

★ **In Letter Parts**
In a friendly letter, a comma is used after the **greeting** and **closing**. In a business letter, a colon follows the greeting.

Dear Aunt Millie,   Sincerely,   Dear Mr. Kelly:

★ **With City, State, and Country**
A comma separates the names of a **city** and **state,** or a **city** and **country.**

How far is Tyler, Texas, from Mexico City, Mexico?

★ **In Dates and Addresses**
A comma is used to separate the **date** from the year. In **addresses,** a comma is used to separate the name of the street and the city and the name of the city and the state.

February 13, 1946, is my grandma's birth date.

I live at 301 Ledge Road, Hudson, Ohio 44067.

Remember:
A colon follows the greeting in a business letter.

★ **In Compound Sentences**

A comma is used before a conjunction to separate two complete thoughts in a **compound sentence**.

Jasmine likes stories, but Eva prefers math.

★ **In a Series**

Commas are used to separate **items in a list** of three or more things.

Rory bought some apples, pears, and oranges.

★ **After Introductory Words and Phrases**

A comma is used after an **introductory word** or **phrase.**

Yes, those are the new members of the team.

Before each game, they need to practice.

★ **With Direct Quotations**

A comma is used to set off a **direct quotation** from the rest of the sentence.

Frank said, "I'm famished."

"I am, too," Eva replied.

★ **With Direct Address**

A comma sets off the **name of a person being spoken to.**

Winnie, you're always ready to work.

★ **With Numbers**

Commas are used with large **numbers** to make them easier to read.

That car has been driven 200,000 miles.

Remember:
Commas often help to make a sentence clearer.

Underlining and Italics

Underlining or **italics** (*slanted type*) is used to identify the titles of books, newspapers, magazines, plays, movies, TV programs, and other long works.

Handwritten titles are underlined; computer-printed titles are shown in italics.

handwritten:	I saw the movie <u>Lost in Space</u>.
computer-printed:	I saw the movie *Lost in Space*.

Stage directions in a play are also set in italics.

BOB: *(Whispering)*   Can you see anything?

Apostrophe

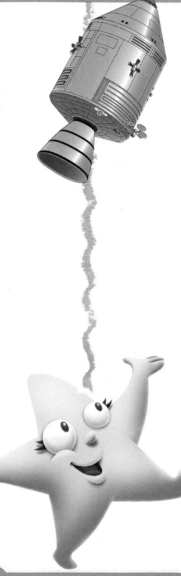

An **apostrophe** is used to signal that letters are missing in a word. It also signals ownership or possession.

★ **In Contractions**

A **contraction** is a shorter word made from two other words. An apostrophe shows where one or more letters have been left out.

did not/didn't   we are/we're   cannot/can't

★ **With Possessive Nouns**

Use an apostrophe followed by the letter *s* (*'s*) to show ownership, or **possession,** for a singular noun. For a plural noun ending in *s*, simply add an apostrophe. For plural nouns not ending in *s*, add an apostrophe and *s*.
▶ **For more help with possessive nouns, see page 249.**

singular:	The astronaut's suit is white and blue.
plural ending in s:	The cosmonauts' new boots are black.
plural not ending in s:	The children's snowsuits are bright blue.

Remember:
Don't use an apostrophe with *his*, *hers*, or *theirs* to show possession.

Quotation marks set off quotations, dialogue, and titles.

★ **In Conversation**
Quotation marks are placed before and after a speaker's exact words.

> Sam asked, "When is the soccer game?"

★ **With Titles of Stories, Poems, and Other Works**
Quotation marks are used before and after titles of stories, poems, magazine articles, songs, and other shorter works.

> I really like Robert Frost's poem "Birches."

A **colon** is used to introduce things, such as a list of items. It is used instead of a comma after the greeting in a business letter. It is also used after each speaker's name in dialogue in a play.

list:	Here is what I need: a hat, a scarf, and gloves.
greeting:	Dear Senator Millhouse:
play:	DAWN: Come to the game on Saturday.

Hyphens are used between words and word parts. Certain compound words also need hyphens. A dictionary will show if a compound word needs a hyphen.

> great-grandparents   smoke-free

▶ For more on hyphens, see syllables, on page 275.

Parentheses set off words that interrupt the flow of a sentence or instructions in a play. They are placed before and after words that give extra information.

> Use the index (pages 291-297) to find the topic you want.

> MARTA: Did you see that? (pointing to door) It moved . . .

Handwriting and Format

Neat handwriting and good penmanship are important to writers. If your handwriting is neat and clear, readers concentrate on your ideas. They won't have to guess at words they can't make out.

When you write a final draft of a letter, article, or story, be sure to write neatly and clearly. Here are letter forms you can use.

$$a\ b\ c\ d\ e\ f\ g\ h\ i\ j\ k\ l\ m\ n$$
$$o\ p\ q\ r\ s\ t\ u\ v\ w\ x\ y\ z$$
$$A\ B\ C\ D\ E\ F\ G\ H\ I\ J\ K\ L\ M$$
$$N\ O\ P\ Q\ R\ S\ T\ U\ V\ W\ X\ Y\ Z$$

Format

How your final draft looks is important. The final draft should be neat and clean. Be careful to not make smudges or cross out words. If necessary, make a clean copy of your writing.

Use lined paper and keep equal margins. Leave one inch margins on the top, sides, and bottom of your paper. Sometimes, you may have to continue a story or a report on a second page.

Write your name on every page. Use the heading your teacher tells you to use.

Remember:
Be proud of what you've written. Make your paper look its very best.

Down the Drain
by Carolyn Reimers

People who waste water are big drips! Every time you leave the water running in the sink you waste gallons of water. Don't wait until a drought happens before saving water. Use water wisely NOW. For example, if you turn off the water while you brush your teeth you save 10 gallons a day. If you fix a leaky faucet you save 100 gallons a day. Use a broom instead of the hose to sweep the sidewalk. Don't use the dishwasher or washing machine until you have a full load. If we all save water we will have water when we really need it. So don't be a big drip. Start saving water now.

Care should be taken to spell words correctly. Misspelled words can make a writer's meaning unclear. Use a dictionary if you are unsure of how to spell a word. Remember that many words in English follow a few simple spelling patterns or rules. Dividing a word into syllables can help you spell it. A **syllable** is a word or part of a word with a single vowel sound.

Syllables in CVC Words

A syllable with a short vowel sound usually follows the consonant-vowel-consonant, or **CVC**, pattern. The vowel comes between two consonants.

pan   pet   hid   hop   cub

man • tle   pen • cil   rib • bon   for • got   cup • ful

Syllables in CVCe Words

A syllable with a long vowel sound often follows the **CVCe** pattern. Adding a final *e* to a CVC word makes the vowel sound long.

pane   Pete   hide   hope   cube

pa • rade   a• maze   ad • vice   hope • less

Use a **hyphen** when you need to divide a word at the end of a writing line. Place the hyphen between syllables.

We found the seeds, took a hand-
ful, and planted them in the garden.

> **Remember:**
> Use hyphens to divide words into syl-la-bles.

Closed and Open Syllables

A **closed syllable** ends in one or more consonants.

pan   pick   hut   help

In a word with two closed syllables, or two consonants in the middle, divide the word between the two consonants.

roc • ket   bas • ket   mar • vel

An **open syllable** ends in a long vowel sound rather than a consonant sound.

pa • per   ho • tel

An **ending** is a letter or group of letters added at the end of a word. Writers add endings to make a word singular or plural or to form other verb tenses.

common endings: s   es   ed   ing

Remember:
Check your endings to be sure you're in the right tense.

Doubling the Final Consonant

Double the final consonant when you add *ed* or *ing* to a one-syllable verb that ends with a short vowel and a consonant.

bat	batted	batting
wrap	wrapped	wrapping

Verbs That End With Two Consonants

If a verb ends with two consonants, such as *lp*, *rt*, and *ck*, do not change the spelling of the verb before adding *s, ed,* or *ing*.

help	helps	helped	helping
start	starts	started	starting

Words That End With *e*

If a verb ends with a consonant-*e* pattern, drop the *e* before adding *es, ed,* or *ing*.

place	places	placed	placing
smile	smiles	smiled	smiling

Add *es* to verbs that end in *ss, sh, ch, x,* or *zz*. Do not change the spelling to add *ed* or *ing*.

press	presses	pressed	pressing
clash	clashes	clashed	clashing
watch	watches	watched	watching
fix	fixes	fixed	fixing
buzz	buzzes	buzzed	buzzing

Verbs ending in *y* and vowel + *y* follow another set of rules when the endings *s, es, ed,* and *ing* are added.

For a verb that ends in a consonant + *y*, change the *y* to *i* when adding the endings *es* and *ed*.

carry	carries	carried
satisfy	satisfies	satisfied
worry	worries	worried

The *y* is not changed to *i* when *ing* is added.

carrying	satisfying	worrying

For most verbs that end in a vowel + *y*, simply add the ending.

obey	obeys	obeyed	obeying
monkey	monkeys	monkeyed	monkeying
enjoy	enjoys	enjoyed	enjoying
display	displays	displayed	displaying

Prefixes

A **prefix** is a word part added to the beginning of a base word, or root. Adding a prefix to a base word forms a new word with a new meaning. Using prefixes expands the number of word choices in writing.

The spelling of the base word, or root, is not changed when a prefix is added.

prefix + base word = new word

pre + view = preview

There are several prefixes that are frequently used. Some of them are listed here with their meanings and the new words formed by joining these prefixes with base words.

Prefix	Meaning	Base Word	New Word
mis	wrong	use	misuse
pre	before	heat	preheat
re	again	start	restart
un	not, absence of	afraid	unafraid

The negative prefixes *im, in, non,* and *un* mean "not" or "opposite of." Always use the dictionary to check the spelling of a word when you are unsure about which of these prefixes to use.

Prefix	Meaning	Base Word	New Word
im	not, opposite of	possible	impossible
in	not, opposite of	ability	inability
non	not, opposite of	stop	nonstop
un	not, opposite of	written	unwritten

Remember:
Pre means "before," so always add a prefix before the base word.

Here are some more often-used prefixes. The spelling of the base word is not changed when the prefixes *de, dis,* and *ex* are added.

Prefix	Meaning	Base Word	New Word
de	**away from, undo**	**plane** **bug**	**deplane** **debug**
dis	**not, opposite of**	**belief** **comfort**	**disbelief** **discomfort**
ex	**from, out of**	**change** **claim**	**exchange** **exclaim**

Adding prefixes to base words can be fun. More importantly, it will reveal a source of "new words" that will be useful to good writers. Here is an example of what can be done with the prefixes *un* and *mis,* using the base word *read.*

Twig says that most people misread bulletin-board messages. I disagree. I think that most bulletin-board messages are unread.

> **Remember:**
> A prefix changes the meaning of a word but not its spelling.

Suffixes

A **suffix** is a word part added at the end of a root word, or base word. Suffixes change how a word is used in a sentence. When added to root words, or base words, suffixes make the words into nouns, verbs, adjectives, or adverbs.

Adding a suffix sometimes changes the spelling of the base word. Generally, the same rules apply to adding suffixes that are used for adding endings. Always check the dictionary when you are unsure of how to spell a word with a suffix.

▶ **For help with adding endings, see pages 276–277.**

> **Remember:**
> Adding a suffix lets you change the way you use a word.

Suffix	Meaning	Base Word	New Word
able	able, can do	wash comfort	washable comfortable
ful	full of	plate hand	plateful handful
less	without	care window	careless windowless
ly	in a manner	friend royal	friendly royally
ness	state of	bright sudden	brightness suddenness
ion	state of	process direct act infect	procession direction action infection

Schwa Sounds

The **schwa sound** is the vowel sound you hear in unaccented syllables. The word *pencil* has the schwa-*l* sound. Schwa-*l* can be spelled in different ways.

schwa *l*: final   wrinkle   panel   civil

A **root**, or base word, is a word to which other word parts can be added. Adding word parts to roots forms new words with new meanings.

think   thinker   unthinkable

common roots: read   speak   help   use

The spelling of the root word does not change when a **prefix** is added in front of it.

un + happy = unhappy

▶ **For help with prefixes, see pages 278–279.**

Adding a **suffix** or **ending** to a root word may change the spelling of a root word.

Rule	Example
No change.	**read + er = reader**
Drop the silent *e* before a vowel.	**mine + er = miner**
Keep the silent *e* before a consonant.	**brave + ly = bravely**
Change *y* to *i* before a consonant.	**happy + ly = happily**
Double the final consonant if the word ends in a vowel plus a consonant.	**stop + able = stoppable**

▶ **For help with endings and suffixes, see pages 276–277 and 280.**

Compound Words

A **compound word** is made of two or more words used together as a new word. There are three kinds of compound words. The dictionary shows how specific compound words are written.

one-word:
speedboat   bluebird
grandstand   needlework
network   newborn

two-word:
rocking chair   junk food
comic book   ice age
district attorney living room

hyphenated:
rock-and-roll   sister-in-law
send-off   blow-dry
well-off   well-to-do

The meaning of a compound word is sometimes different from the meaning of the individual words that make up the compound. A compound word should be used with its proper meaning.

Remember:
The parts of a compound word make up a single new word.

Homonyms are words that sound alike but have different meanings and different spellings. Some sound-alike words can cause special problems because each one is used in a different way in a sentence. The spelling of a homonym should match the meaning that is right for the sentence.

★ **to/too/two**

preposition:	I talk to my dad often.
adverb:	Eve has a brother, too.
number:	My two sisters are teenagers.

★ **our/hour**

possessive pronoun:	Our clock is slow.
noun:	We waited an hour for him.

★ **stare/stair**

verb:	It is impolite to stare.
noun:	That stair is broken.

★ **they're/their/there**

contraction:	They're (they are) going now.
possessive pronoun:	The boys found their books.
adverb:	We live there.

Remember:
Their doesn't mean *there* or *they're*. They're all used differently and spelled differently, too.

★ **you're/your**

contraction:	You're (you are) a good friend.
possessive pronoun:	Where is your library card?

★ **it's/its**

contraction:	It's (it is) still daylight.
possessive pronoun:	Our dog enjoys its food.

Synonyms

A **synonym** is a word that has almost the same meaning as another word. Sometimes a word has just the right meaning for a sentence.

The spinning motion made Lisa dizzy.

The spinning motion made Lisa unsteady.

Often a word has more than one synonym.

Brad paddled a canoe across the placid lake.

Brad paddled a canoe across the calm lake.

Brad paddled a canoe across the peaceful lake.

Remember:
A synonym or antonym of a word rarely has exactly the same or opposite meaning.

Antonyms

An **antonym** is a word that is almost opposite in meaning to another word. Antonyms can help you express differences clearly.

Tess always wore fancy boots to parties.

Tess did not own any plain boots.

Often a word has more than one antonym. For example, several antonyms for the word *cautious* are shown in these sentences.

Jamal plays a daring game of chess.

Jamal plays a fearless game of chess.

Jamal plays a bold game of chess.

A thesaurus provides a choice of synonyms and antonyms for many words.

▶ **For help in using a thesaurus, see page 286.**

A **dictionary** is one of a writer's best tools. Use it often to be sure you know how to use, pronounce, and spell thousands of words.

Dictionary

At the top of every dictionary page is a pair of **guide words**. These words tell you the first and last words on the page. Any word that comes between these two words in alphabetical order will be on that page.

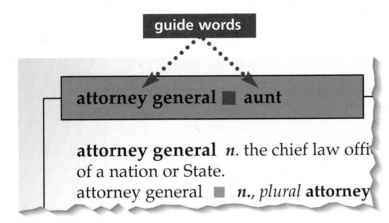

guide words

attorney general ■ **aunt**

attorney general *n.* the chief law offi of a nation or State.
attorney general ■ *n., plural* **attorney**

Each word that is defined in the dictionary is called an **entry word**. Notice all the things the dictionary tells you about an entry word.

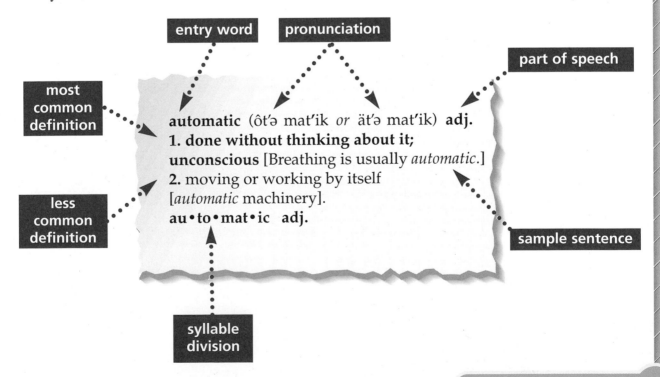

entry word

pronunciation

part of speech

most common definition

automatic (ôt′ə mat′ik *or* ät′ə mat′ik) **adj.**
1. done without thinking about it; unconscious [Breathing is usually *automatic.*]
2. moving or working by itself [*automatic* machinery].
au•to•mat•ic adj.

less common definition

sample sentence

syllable division

Thesaurus

When you revise your work, you often need a more exact or interesting word. A **thesaurus** is a useful tool for this. It is your best source of synonyms, or words with similar meanings.

Like a dictionary, a thesaurus has entries listed in alphabetical order. Each entry word has a label showing the part of speech. After this label is a list of synonyms. The entry may also give sample sentences and antonyms, words that mean the opposite of the entry word.

enormous adj. colossal, gigantic, huge, immense, mammoth, massive, vast.

These words share the meaning "extremely large."

- What enormous ears!
- We saw a colossal statue of Christopher Columbus.
- We ate a gigantic dinner.
- Great Danes are huge dogs.
- There are immense forests in the United States.
- New York is a mammoth city.
- Massive steel beams support the skyscraper.
- We saw vast icebergs from the ship.

antonym: tiny

Whenever you revise your writing, try to use a thesaurus. If you are using a word-processing program on your school or home computer, you can also use the built-in thesaurus. This feature makes changing words very easy.

Remember:
Try out different words in your sentence. Choose the one that sounds best and makes the most sense.

An **encyclopedia** is a book or set of books that gives information about different subjects. Each **volume,** or book, is made up of articles that are arranged in alphabetical order.

If there is more than one volume, each one usually has a number on the spine, or back. Each volume also usually has a guide word or two to let you know what words will be found on the pages.

In a library, some encyclopedias are about a single topic, such as "science" or "plants" or "space." Other encyclopedias are general and cover many varied topics. When you need information from one of these works, it may be helpful to talk with your teacher or a librarian first. Choosing the encyclopedia that is the best one to use may take practice.

The pages of an encyclopedia are like those of a dictionary, with **guide words** at the top of the page and **entry words** on the rest of the page.

The encyclopedia's entry words are like the keywords you single out in your research topic. If you are investigating **photosynthesis**, for example, look in the volume for the letter *p.* Then use the guide words to find the entry *photosynthesis.*

Many encyclopedia articles have photographs, charts, or maps. These often have important information about a topic. Remember to read the titles and captions of these graphic aids carefully. They often have just the fact you might be looking for!

Remember:
Knowing the keyword to use is the first step in getting information from an encyclopedia.

Electronic Encyclopedias

Encyclopedias are also available on CD-ROMs and on the Internet. These electronic versions save space on library and home bookshelves and present topics with audio and video.

For example, an article about Mozart may include an audio example of one of his well-known works. A photosynthesis entry may provide a video showing the process of photosynthesis.

You will find that locating information in these electronic encyclopedias is quite easy. Often, you have to do nothing more than type a topic or entry word. Then, you simply have to choose exactly which pieces of information you want to read, hear, or watch.

Internet

Today, the **Internet** is a popular source of information. Many Web sites, though, give out information that is not carefully checked and may not be completely accurate. Furthermore, some Web sites deliberately select or even change facts in order to present a particular point of view. It is important to be aware of this whenever you look for and use Internet information.

The best way to do research on the Internet is to visit reliable Web sites. Teachers and librarians often can suggest good sites to use. They also can suggest guide books that can lead you to good Web sites.

Remember:
Teachers, librarians, and guide books can lead you to Web sites you can trust.

An **atlas** is a book of maps. A good desk-sized world atlas also may contain information about climate, land formations, populations, cultures, and politics.

On many maps, you will see a **compass rose**. This usually is a cross with an arrow pointing north. It helps to identify the directions north (N), south (S), east (E), and west (W).

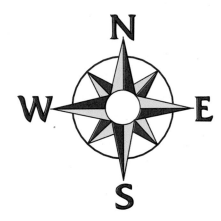

When you are studying a map, it is important to understand the relationship between distance on the map and distance on the earth's surface. That relationship is called the **scale**. It can differ widely on different maps. Mapmakers usually provide a **distance scale**, which is a line that has been marked at set spaces, much like a ruler.

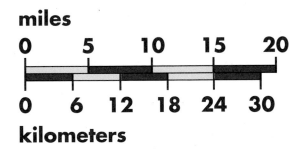

You can determine actual distance between two cities (points on a map) by measuring the distance between them on the map. Then compare that distance with the distance marked along the distance scale.

Like other reference resources, atlases are published on CD-ROMs and can be downloaded from the Internet.

Almanac

An **almanac** is filled with facts, figures, charts, and other information. Almanacs are published every year and have information on dozens of subjects, from facts about the United States and foreign countries to lists of World Series and Oscar winners.

Because a new almanac is published each year, it is a good source of updated information on a wide range of topics. Almanacs usually have facts and figures about these main topics.

- Important Events of the Previous Year
- Consumer Information
- Economics
- Health
- Language, Arts, and Media
- Nations of the World
- People
- Religion
- Science and Technology
- Sports
- Transportation
- United States
- World History and Geography

When you want to find information about a particular topic, always look in the index. This can be found in the back of most almanacs. Some almanacs, though, provide an index at the front of the book. The index will direct you to the correct page in the book.

Remember:
An almanac is a good source for up-to-date information.

Index

Art & Photo Credits

Illustrations: Front cover, pencilperson, starperson: Bernard Adnet. iii: Peter Fasolino. iv: *t.* Peter Fasolino; *m.* Eldon Doty; *b.l.*, *b.r.* Ken Edwards. v: *t.* Mike Lester; *m.r.* David Scanlan; *b.r.* Daniel Vasconcellos. 2: Dee Deloy. 5, 7: Bonnie Matthews. 8: Kelly Kennedy. 9: Bonnie Matthews. 10–11: Kelly Kennedy. 15: Randy Verougstraete. 16: Todd Nordling. 21, 22, 23, 25, 27, 28, 29, 30, 31, 33, 34: Peter Fasolino. 36: Bernard Adnet. 37: Bonnie Matthews. 38–39, 40: Bob Byrd. 41: Giovannina Colalillo. 42–43: Bryan Haynes. 44, 45: Tim Sposato. 47: Eldon Doty. 49: Bernard Adnet. 50–51: Thomas Buchs. 52, 53, 54: Olivia McElroy. 56, 66: Diana Magnuson. 69, 71, 72: Lane DuPont. 73, 74, 75, 76, 77, 78, 79, 80, 81, 82–83, 84, 85, 86: Ken Edwards. 88, 90, 91: Chris Van Es. 93, 94, 95, 96: David Merrell. 97: Bernard Adnet. 98–99: Ronald Finger. 100, 101, 103, 104: Rosanne Kaloustian. 105, 106–107, 108–109, 110–111, 112–113, 114: Bob Dombrowski. 116, 117, 118: Diana Magnuson. 119, 120–121: Mike Lester. 133: Bernard Adnet. 134, 135, 136: David Scanlan. 139, 141, 142, 143, 144, 145, 146, 147, 148: Leslie Wu. 150, 151, 152, 153, 154: Grace DeVito. 155, 157, 158, 159, 160, 161, 166, 169, 173, 174, 175: Bill Scott. 180, 181, 182: Gail Piazza. 183: Bernard Adnet. 184, 185: Stephen Foster. 186, 187, 188: Jeff Seaver. 189, 190, 191, 192–193, 194, 195, 197, 198: Gregg Valley. 202, 204: Mary O'Keefe Young. 205, 206, 207, 208, 209, 210, 211, 212, 213: Daniel Vasconcellos. 217: Diane Bigda.

Photos: All photos ©Modern Curriculum Press unless otherwise noted.
v: *m.l.* Michael Provost for Modern Curriculum Press. 26–27, 28: David Young-Wolff/PhotoEdit. 30: Corbis-Bettman. 47: *t.* Astronaut Suit Courtesy of U.S. Space Camp®; *b.l.* T. Kitchin/Tom Stack & Associates; *b.r.* Phil Degginger/Tony Stone Images. 55, 66, 67*t.*: Charles Turner for Modern Curriculum Press. 68: Favorite Scary Stories of American Children, by Richard & Judy Dockrey Young, Illustrated by Wendell E. Hall, Published by August House, Inc. ©1990. 73, 86, 87*t.*: Davis Barber for Modern Curriculum Press. 88: The Illustrated Book of Myths, Retold by Neil Philip, Illustrated by Nilesh Mistry, Published by Dorling Kindersley Limited, London. 92: How To Eat Fried Worms, by Thomas Rockwell, Illustrated by Emily McGully, Published by Bantam Doubleday Dell Books ©1973. 102: *t.* The Random House Book of Poetry for Children, Selected by Jack Prelutsky, Illustrated by Arnold Lobel, Published by Random House ©1983; *b.* Matilde Champagne. 105, 114, 115*t.*: Richard Nowitz for Modern Curriculum Press. 119, 120, 128: Gregory Phelps for Modern Curriculum Press. 130: *t.l.* Earth Shine, by Anne Morrow Lindbergh, Published by Hartcourt Brace & World, Inc. ©1966; *r.* NASA; *b.l.* UPI/Corbis-Bettmann. 132: NASA. 136: *t.l.* National Geographic Society; *b.l.* Courtesy of Julie Agnone. 139, 140, 148, 149*t.*: Michael Provost for Modern Curriculum Press. 163, 164–165, 167, 168, 170–171, 175: NASA. 176 sunset: PhotoDisc, Inc. 177: *l.* PhotoDisc, Inc.; *r.* Girls' Life Magazine. 178: *t.r.* PhotoDisc, Inc. 179: *t.l.* PhotoDisc, Inc.; *b.* Silver Burdett Ginn. 186: *l.* Courtesy of Texas Medical Association. 189: *l.* Twentieth Century Fox/Photofest. 200: I Have a Dream, by Dr. Martin Luther King, Jr., Published by Scholastic Inc. 201: UPI/Corbis-Bettmann. 205, 206, 214, 215*t.*: Nancy Ferguson for Modern Curriculum Press. 222: Silver Burdett Ginn. 226: Jade Albert for Silver Burdett Ginn. 231, 235, 242, 246, 254, 258, 262, 266, 268: Silver Burdett Ginn. 271: Elliott Smith for Silver Burdett Ginn. 275, 279, 283, 287: Silver Burdett Ginn.